marketing
3.0

marketing 3.0

From Products to
Customers to
the Human
Spirit

PHILIP KOTLER

HERMAWAN KARTAJAYA   IWAN SETIAWAN

WILEY

JOHN WILEY & SONS, INC.

For general information on our other products and services or for technical support, please contact our Customer Care Department within the United States at (800) 762-2974, outside the United States at (317) 572-3993 or fax (317) 572-4002.

Wiley also publishes its books in a variety of electronic formats. Some content that appears in print may not be available in electronic books. For more information about Wiley products, visit our web site at www.wiley.com.

ISBN 978-0-470-59882-5

Printed in the United States of America.

10 9 8 7 6 5 4 3 2 1

"To the next generation of Marketers who will enhance the social and environmental contributions of the marketing discipline."
Philip Kotler

"To my first grandson, Darren Hermawan, The Next Great Marketer."
Hermawan Kartajaya

"To Louise for her endless support."
Iwan Setiawan

CONTENTS

PART III
Application

FOREWORD

According to Alvin Toffler, human civilization can be divided into three waves of the economy. The first wave is the Agriculture Age, in which the most important capital is the land for agriculture. My country, Indonesia, is undoubtedly rich in this type of capital. The second is the Industrial Age following the Industrial Revolution in England and the rest of Europe. The essential kinds of capital in this age are machines and the factory. The third era is the Information Age, where mind, information, and high tech are the imperative types of capital to succeed. Today, as humanity embraces the challenge of global warming, we are moving toward the fourth wave, which is oriented to creativity, culture, heritage, and the environment. In leading Indonesia, this is my future direction.

When I read this book, I could see that marketing is also moving toward the same direction. Marketing 3.0 relies heavily on the marketers' ability to sense human anxieties and desires, which are rooted in creativity, culture, heritage, and the environment. This is even more relevant for Indonesia because the country is known for its diversity in culture and heritage. Indonesia is also a very values-driven country. Spirituality has always been the central part of our lives.

I am happy with the examples in the book of successful multinational companies that support Millenium Development Goals for reducing poverty and unemployment in developing countries. I believe that public-private partnership has always been a strong fundamental for economic growth, especially in a developing country. This book is also very supportive for my mission to shift poor people at the bottom of the pyramid in Indonesia to the middle of the pyramid. It also supports the nation's efforts to preserve the environment as our strongest asset.

In summary, I am proud to have two renowned marketing gurus putting their energy and effort into writing a book for a better world. Congratulations for Philip Kotler, Hermawan Kartajaya, and Iwan Setiawan for this mind-stimulating book. I hope that anyone who reads this book will be encouraged to make a difference in the world we are living in.

—Susilo Bambang Yudhoyono
President of the Republic of Indonesia

PREFACE

The world is going through a period of rapid and wrenching changes. The recent financial meltdown has unfortunately increased the level of poverty and unemployment, developments that are now being fought with stimulus packages around the world to restore confidence and economic growth. In addition, climate change and rising pollution are challenging countries to limit the release of carbon dioxide into the atmosphere, but at the cost of imposing a higher burden on business. Furthermore, the rich countries of the West are now experiencing a much slower rate of growth, and economic power is rapidly shifting to countries in the East that are experiencing higher rates of growth. And finally, technology is shifting from the mechanical world to the digital world—the Internet, computers, cell phones, and social media—which is having a profound impact on the behavior of producers and consumers.

These and other changes will require a major rethinking of marketing. The concept of marketing can be seen as the balancing concept to that of macroeconomics. Whenever the macroeconomic environment changes, so will consumer behavior change, and this will lead marketing to change. Over the past 60 years, marketing has moved from being product-centric (Marketing 1.0) to being consumer-centric (Marketing 2.0). Today we see marketing as transforming once again in response to the new dynamics in the environment. We see companies expanding their focus from products to consumers to humankind issues. Marketing 3.0 is the stage when companies shift from consumer-centricity to human-centricity and where profitability is balanced with corporate responsibility.

We see a company not as a sole and self-sustaining operator in a competitive world but as a company that operates with a loyal network of partners—employees, distributors, dealers, and suppliers. If the company chooses its network partners carefully, and their goals are aligned and the rewards are equitable and motivating, the company and its partners combined will become a powerful competitor. To achieve this, the company must share its mission, vision, and values with its team members so that they act in unison to achieve their goals.

We describe in this book how a company can market its mission, vision, and values to each of its major stakeholders. The company gets its profits by creating superior value for its customers and stakeholder partners. We hope that the company views its customers as its strategic starting point and wants to address them in their full humanity and with attention to their needs and concerns.

The book is structured into three key parts. In Part I, we summarize the key business trends that shape the human-centric marketing imperative and lay the foundation for Marketing 3.0. In Part II, we show how the company can market its corporate vision, mission, and values to each of its key stakeholders—consumers, employees, channel partners, and shareholders. In Part III, we share their thoughts on several key implementations of Marketing 3.0 for solving global issues such as wellness, poverty, and environmental sustainability and how corporations can contribute by implementing the human-centric business model. Finally, the Epilogue chapter summarizes the 10 key ideas of Marketing 3.0 with select examples of companies that embrace the concept in their business model.

NOTE ON THE ORIGIN OF THIS BOOK

The idea of Marketing 3.0 was first conceptualized in Asia back in November 2005 by a group of consultants at

MarkPlus, a Southeast Asian–based marketing services firm led by Hermawan Kartajaya. After two years of co-creation to enhance the concept, Philip Kotler and Hermawan Kartajaya launched the draft manuscript at the 40th anniversary of the Association of Southeast Asian Nations (ASEAN) in Jakarta. The only G-20 member in Southeast Asia, Indonesia is a nation where human centricity and the character of spirituality overcome the challenges of diversity. The president of the United States, Barack Obama, spent four years of his early education in Indonesia to learn about the human centricity of the East. Marketing 3.0 was born and shaped in the East, and we are honored to have a Foreword by Susilo Bambang Yudhoyono, President of the Republic of Indonesia.

Iwan Setiawan, one of the MarkPlus consultants who initiated the concept, collaborated with Philip Kotler at Northwestern University's Kellogg School of Management—one of the world's top business schools in the West—to enhance the relevance of Marketing 3.0 with the emergence of the new world economic order and the rise of the digital world.

ABOUT THE AUTHORS

Philip Kotler, the S.C. Johnson & Son Distinguished Professor of International Marketing at the Kellogg School of Management, Northwestern University, is also widely regarded as the Father of Modern Marketing. He is ranked by the *Wall Street Journal* as one of the top six most influential business thinkers.

Hermawan Kartajaya is the founder and CEO of MarkPlus, Inc., and is one of the "50 Gurus Who Have Shaped the Future of Marketing," according to the Chartered Institute of Marketing, United Kingdom.

Iwan Setiawan (Kellogg School of Management 2010) is a senior consultant at MarkPlus, Inc.

PART I

TRENDS

CHAPTER ONE

Welcome to Marketing 3.0

WHY MARKETING 3.0?

Over the years, marketing has evolved through three stages that we call Marketing 1.0, 2.0, and 3.0. Many of today's marketers still practice Marketing 1.0, some practice Marketing 2.0, and a few are moving into Marketing 3.0. The greatest opportunities will come to marketers practicing 3.0.

Long ago, during the industrial age—when the core technology was industrial machinery—marketing was about selling the factory's output of products to all who would buy them. The products were fairly basic and were designed to serve a mass market. The goal was to standardize and scale up to bring about the lowest possible costs of production so that these goods could be priced lower and made more affordable to more buyers. Henry Ford's Model T automobile epitomized this strategy; said Ford: "Any customer can have a car painted any color that he wants so long as it is black." This was Marketing 1.0 or the product-centric era.

Marketing 2.0 came out in today's information age—where the core is information technology. The job of marketing is no longer that simple. Today's consumers are well informed and can easily compare several similar product offerings. The product value is defined by the consumer. Consumers differ greatly in their preferences. The marketer must segment the market and develop a superior product for a specific target market. The golden rule of "customer is king" works well for most companies. Consumers are better off because their needs and wants are well addressed. They can choose from a wide range of functional characteristics and alternatives. Today's marketers try to touch the consumer's mind and heart. Unfortunately, the consumer-centric approach implicitly assumes the view that consumers are passive targets of marketing campaigns. This is the view in Marketing 2.0 or the customer-oriented era.

Now, we are witnessing the rise of Marketing 3.0 or the values-driven era. Instead of treating people simply as consumers, marketers approach them as whole human beings with minds, hearts, and spirits. Increasingly, consumers are looking for solutions to their anxieties about making the globalized world a better place. In a world full of confusion, they search for companies that address their deepest needs for social, economic, and environmental justice in their mission, vision, and values. They look for not only functional and emotional fulfillment but also human spirit fulfillment in the products and services they choose.

Like consumer-oriented Marketing 2.0, Marketing 3.0 also aims to satisfy the consumer. However, companies practicing Marketing 3.0 have bigger missions, visions, and values to contribute to the world; they aim to provide solutions to address problems in the society. Marketing 3.0 lifts the concept of marketing into the arena of human aspirations, values, and spirit. Marketing 3.0 believes that consumers are complete human beings whose other needs and hopes should never be neglected. Therefore, Marketing 3.0 complements emotional marketing with human spirit marketing.

In times of global economic crisis, Marketing 3.0 gains more relevance to the lives of the consumers as they are impacted more by rapid social, economic, and environmental change and turbulence. Diseases become pandemics, poverty increases, and environmental destruction is under way. Companies practicing Marketing 3.0 provide answers and hope to people confronting such issues and, therefore, touch consumers at a higher level. In Marketing 3.0, companies differentiate themselves by their values. In turbulent times, this differentiation is arguably a strong one.

Table 1.1 summarizes the comparison of Marketing 1.0, 2.0, and 3.0 from comprehensive viewpoints.

To understand Marketing 3.0 better, let us examine the rise of three major forces that shape the business landscape toward Marketing 3.0: the age of participation, the age of globalization paradox, and the age of creative society. Observe how these three major forces transform consumers to be more collaborative, cultural, and human spirit-driven. Understanding this transformation will lead to a better understanding of Marketing 3.0 as a nexus of collaborative, cultural, and spiritual marketing.

THE AGE OF PARTICIPATION AND COLLABORATIVE MARKETING

Technological advances have brought about huge changes in consumers, markets, and marketing over the past century. Marketing 1.0 was initiated by production technology development during the Industrial Revolution. Marketing 2.0 came into being as a result of information technology and the Internet. Now, new wave technology becomes the major driver for the birth of Marketing 3.0.

Since early 2000, information technology has penetrated the mainstream market and further developed into what is considered the new wave technology. New wave technology is technology that enables connectivity and interactivity of individuals and groups. New wave technology consists of three major forces: cheap computers and mobile phones, low-cost Internet, and open source.[1] The technology allows individuals to express themselves and collaborate with others. The emergence of new wave technology marks the era that

Table 1.1 Comparison of Marketing 1.0, 2.0, and 3.0

	Marketing 1.0 Product-centric Marketing	Marketing 2.0 Consumer-oriented Marketing	Marketing 3.0 Values-driven Marketing
Objective	Sell products	Satisfy and retain the consumers	Make the world a better place
Enabling forces	Industrial Revolution	Information technology	New wave technology
How companies see the market	Mass buyers with physical needs	Smarter consumer with mind and heart	Whole human with mind, heart, and spirit
Key marketing concept	Product development	Differentiation	Values
Company marketing guidelines	Product specification	Corporate and product positioning	Corporate mission, vision, and values
Value propositions	Functional	Functional and emotional	Functional, emotional, and spiritual
Interaction with consumers	One-to-many transaction	One-to-one relationship	Many-to-many collaboration

Scott McNealy, Chairman of Sun Microsystems, declared as the age of participation. In the age of participation, people create news, ideas, and entertainment as well as consume them. New wave technology enables people to turn from being consumers into prosumers.

One of the enablers of new wave technology is the rise of social media. We classify social media in two broad categories. One is the *expressive* social media, which includes blogs, Twitter, YouTube, Facebook, photo sharing sites like Flickr, and other social networking sites. The other category is the *collaborative* media, which includes sites such as Wikipedia, Rotten Tomatoes, and Craigslist.

Expressive Social Media

Let us examine the impact of expressive social media on marketing. In early 2008, Technorati found 13 million active blogs around the world.[2] As with readership of print media, readership of blogs varies among countries. Unlike in Japan where 74 percent of Internet users read blogs, only around 27 percent of Internet users in the United States read blogs. Although the readership is low, 34 percent of blog readers in the United States are influencers. As a result, U.S. blogs stimulate follow-up actions by 28 percent of their readers.[3] Seth Godin, a well-known marketer, runs a popular web site that offers a new idea every day to influence thousands of people who have elected to receive his feed.

Another popular form of blogging, and one of the fastest growing forms of social media is Twitter. From April 2008 to April 2009, the number of Twitter users has grown 1,298 percent.[4] The microblogging site allows members to broadcast tweets of 140 characters or fewer to their followers. It is considered much simpler than blogging because users can easily send tweets from handheld devices such as iPhones and Blackberrys. Through Twitter, users can share their thoughts, their activities, and even their moods with friends or fans. Actor Ashton Kutcher reportedly hit the 1 million followers mark on Twitter, beating out even CNN.

Many of the blogs and tweets are personal where a person shares news, opinion, and ideas with chosen others. Another set of blogs and tweets are set up by persons who want to comment on the news or offer opinions and small essays on anything crossing their minds. Other bloggers or twitterers might comment on companies and products, supporting them or criticizing them. An angry blogger or twitterer with a widespread audience has the potential to dissuade many consumers from wanting to do business with a particular company or organization.

The popularity of blogging and twittering has reached the corporate world. IBM, for example, encourages its employees to create their own blogs where they can talk freely about their company as long as they adhere to certain guidelines. Another example is General Electric, which established a Tweet Squad, a group of young employees who train older employees to use social media.

People are also creating short video clips and sending them to YouTube for the world to see. Many are aspiring filmmakers who hope their creativity will be recognized and lead to broader opportunities. Other video clips are prepared by organizations to enlist support for or against some cause or activity. Still other video clips are prepared by companies to dramatize their products and service offerings. One high-profile campaign on YouTube was Marc Ecko's *Air Force One* hoax. To demonstrate its affinity for graffiti art, the clothing company made a video that showed a couple of youngsters spraying the words "Still Free" on *Air Force One*. It later admitted that the plane on the video was not *Air Force One* and it just wanted to create a pop-culture sensation as part of its brand–building efforts on YouTube.

As social media becomes increasingly expressive, consumers will be able to increasingly influence other consumers with their opinions and experiences. The influence that corporate advertising has on shaping buying behavior will diminish accordingly. In addition, consumers are getting more involved in other activities such as video games, watching DVDs, using the computer, and they are watching fewer ads.

Because social media is low-cost and bias-free, it will be the future for marketing communications. Connections between friends on social networking sites such as Facebook and MySpace can also help companies gain insights into the market. Researchers at IBM, Hewlett-Packard, and Microsoft are mining social networking data to do profiling and design better communication approaches for their employees and consumers.[5]

Collaborative Social Media

Consider also collaborative social media that applies open sourcing. A decade ago, people knew that software could be open sourced and developed collaboratively. People knew Linux. However, no one considered that this kind of collaboration could be applied to other industries. Who would have imagined an encyclopedia that anyone can edit like Wikipedia?

Wikipedia's content is contributed to by vast numbers of people who volunteer their time to create entries on countless topics for this community-built encyclopedia. By mid-2009, Wikipedia had developed 235 active language editions with more than 13 million articles (2.9 million in English).[6] Compare this with *We Are Smarter than Me*, a book written by thousands of people. The book is an example of collaboration in traditional book publishing.[7] Another example is Craigslist, which aggregates and displays millions of classified ads for free, posing a threat to newspapers that sell advertising space. Owned partly by eBay, the site also becomes the marketplace for a large number of communities placing ads to sell and buy various items.

Collaboration can also be the new source of innovation. In *Open Business Models*, Chesbrough explained how companies can use crowdsourcing to find new ideas and solutions.[8] A company called InnoCentive broadcasts research and development challenges and solicits the best solutions. It welcomes companies that wish to find solutions to their problems (solution seekers) and also individuals, scientists, and researchers who can propose solutions to the problems (problem solvers). Once the best solution is found, InnoCentive will ask the solution seeker to give a cash incentive to the problem solver. Like Wikipedia and Craigslist, InnoCentive becomes a marketplace that facilitates collaboration. This mass collaboration phenomenon is described by Tapscott and Williams in their book, *Wikinomics*.[9]

The growing trend toward collaborative consumers has affected business. Marketers today no longer have full control over their brands because they are now competing with the collective power of consumers. This growing trend of consumers taking over the job of marketers is what Wipperfürth anticipated in *Brand Hijack*.[10] Companies must now collaborate with their consumers. Collaboration begins when marketing managers listen to the consumers' voices to understand their minds and capture market insights. A more advanced collaboration takes place when consumers themselves play the key role in creating value through cocreation of products and services.

Trendwatching, a large trend research network, summarizes consumers' motivation for product co-creation. Some consumers enjoy demonstrating their abilities in value-creation for everyone to see. Some consumers want to tailor a product or service to their specific lifestyles. Sometimes, consumers target reward money given by companies for co-creation efforts. Others see co-creation as an opportunity to secure employment. There are also people who undertake cocreation just for fun.[11]

Procter & Gamble (P&G) is known for its connect and develop strategy, which replaces its traditional research and development approach. The P&G model resembles a starfish, which, according to Brafman and Beckstrom, is a good metaphor for companies of the future because it has no head and is more like groups of cells working together.[12] The open innovation program leverages P&G's network of entrepreneurs and suppliers around the world to provide fresh and innovative product ideas. The program contributes around 35 percent of P&G's revenue.[13] Some of the well-known products invented through connect and develop include Olay Regenerist, Swiffer Dusters, and the Crest SpinBrush. The program proves that collaboration can work in industries other than information technology.

Besides helping companies to develop products, consumers can also contribute ideas for advertising. Consider the "Free Doritos" advertisement. The user-generated ad won the top spot at the 21st Annual USA Today Super Bowl Ad Meter, defeating ads made by professional agencies. The victory proved that user-generated content can often reach consumers better because it is more relevant and more accessible.

This increase in consumer participation and collaboration is examined in *The Future of Competition*.[14] Authors Prahalad and Ramaswamy argue that consumer roles are changing. Consumers are no longer isolated individuals, rather they are connected with one another. In making decisions, they are no longer unaware but are informed. They are no longer passive but are active in giving useful feedback to companies.

Therefore marketing evolved. In the first stage, marketing was transaction oriented, focused on how to make a sale. In the second stage, marketing became relationship oriented, how to keep a consumer coming back and buying more. In the third stage, marketing has shifted to inviting consumers to participate in the company's development of products and communications.

Collaborative marketing is the first building block of Marketing 3.0. Companies practicing Marketing 3.0 aim to change the world. They cannot do it alone. In the interlinked economy, they must collaborate with one another, with their shareholders, with their channel partners, with their employees, and with their consumers. Marketing 3.0 is a collaboration of business entities with similar sets of values and desires.

THE AGE OF GLOBALIZATION PARADOX AND CULTURAL MARKETING

Besides the impact of technology on shaping new consumer attitudes toward Marketing 3.0, another major force has been globalization. Globalization is driven by technology. Information technology enables the exchange of information among nations, corporations, and individuals around the world, while transportation technology facilitates trade and other physical exchange in global value chains. Like technology, globalization reaches everyone around the world and creates an interlinked economy. But unlike technology, globalization is a force that stimulates counterbalance. In search of the right balance, globalization often creates paradoxes.

Consider the year 1989, which symbolized the rise of the globalization paradox. In 1989, the Chinese government used its military strength to put down a protest in Tiananmen Square. A series of pro-democracy demonstrations led by students, intellectuals, and labor activists resulted in a military crackdown that left between 400 and 800 civilians dead and between 7,000 and 10,000 injured. In the same year in Europe, another historical event occurred. The Berlin Wall, which had separated West Germany from East Germany, was knocked down, laying to rest a tangible symbol of the Cold War. David Hasselhoff, standing on the Berlin Wall, performed his popular song "Looking for Freedom." The two 1989 events are paradoxical events. The Tiananmen Square event marked the fall of the pro-democracy movement in China, which halted movement toward freedom, while the dismantling of the Berlin Wall represented the beginning of a new world of freedom and democracy. Globalization liberates but at the same time puts pressure on nations and people around the world.

Consider, also, the two opposing views of Thomas Friedman and Robert Samuelson, representing globalization and nationalism, respectively. On the one hand, Friedman argued in *The World Is Flat*[15] that the world is now without borders. The flow of goods, services, and people can move seamlessly because of cheap transportation and information technology. On the other hand, Samuelson argued in his article, "The World Is Still Round,"[16] that national borders will remain because they are driven by politics and psychology. Globalization levels the playing field for nations around the world, but at the same time it threatens them. Consequently, countries will defend their national markets against globalization. In other words, globalization provokes nationalism.

Globalization is indeed full of paradoxes. We can list at least three macro paradoxes that arise as a result of globalization. First, while democracy is finding more global roots, the new, nondemocratic superpower, China, grows in power. China has become the world's factory and holds a key role in the global economy. Despite the growing influence of democracy in the world, the cash-rich nation proves that capitalism does not require democracy. Globalization may open up the economy but not the politics. The political landscape remains national. This is the political paradox of globalization.

Second, globalization calls for economic integration but does not create equal economies. As Joseph Stiglitz argued in *Globalization and Its Discontents*, the processes of privatization, liberalization, and stabilization have been mismanaged, and therefore many third world countries and former Communist states are actually worse off now than they were before. Economically, globalization appears to hurt as many countries as it helps. Even within the same nation, unequal wealth distribution exists. Today, there are millions of affluent people around the world. India has more than 50 billionaires. The average CEO in the United States earns 400 times that of the average employee. Unfortunately, there are still more than 1 billion people in the world who live in the state of extreme poverty and subsist on less than $1 a day. This is the economic paradox of globalization.

Third, globalization creates not a uniform but a diverse culture. In 1996, Benjamin Barber wrote *Jihad vs. McWorld: How Globalism and Tribalism Are Reshaping the World* in which he asserts that there are two axial and opposing principles of our age: tribalism and globalism.[17] In 2000, in *The Lexus and the Olive Tree: Understanding Globalization*,[18] Thomas Friedman wrote about the clash of the globalization system, symbolized by the Lexus, and ancient forces of culture, geography, tradition, and community symbolized by the olive tree. Globalization creates universal global culture while at the same time strengthens traditional culture as a counterbalance. This is the sociocultural paradox of globalization, which has the most direct impact on individuals or consumers.

This list of paradoxes is far from exhaustive—there are a lot more than three paradoxes—but it is sufficient to describe why consumer behavior changes in globalization and why Marketing 3.0 is required to capture the trends. Thanks to technology, these globalization paradoxes, especially the sociocultural paradox, influence not only nations and corporations but also individuals. Individuals have started to feel the pressure of becoming global citizens as well as local citizens. As a result, many people are anxious and carry conflicting intertwined values in their minds. Especially in times of economic turbulence, anxiety increases. Many people blame globalization as the cause of the global economic crisis.

Author Charles Handy suggests that people should not try to solve these paradoxes but rather try to manage them.[19] To do that, people reach for a sense of continuity in their lives. People search for connection with others. People begin to blend into their local community and society. Yet a sense of direction is also essential in times of paradox as people start to join together to support social causes such as Habitat for Humanity or the Sierra Club. In this case, globalization has a positive impact on our lives. Paradoxes lead to a greater awareness and concern about poverty, injustice, environmental sustainability, community responsibility, and social purpose.

A major effect of these paradoxes of globalization is that companies are now competing to be seen as providing continuity, connection, and direction. According to Holt, cultural brands aim to resolve paradoxes in society. They can address social, economic, and environmental issues in the society. Because they address the collective anxieties and desires of a nation, cultural brands often have high equity.[20]

Cultural brands need to be dynamic because they tend to be relevant only at a certain period of time when certain contradictions are evident in the society. Therefore, cultural brands should always be aware of new emerging paradoxes that are changing over time. In the 1970s, Coca-Cola created an advertisement featuring the song, "I'd Like to Teach the World to Sing." At that time, it was relevant because U.S. society was divided in its support of the Vietnam War. Today, it would no longer be as relevant, although people will always remember the cultural campaign.

To develop such a culturally relevant campaign, marketers must understand something about anthropology and sociology. They should be able to recognize cultural paradoxes that might not be obvious. This is difficult to do because cultural paradoxes are not something that people typically talk about. Consumers who are affected by cultural campaigns are a majority but they are the silent majority. They sense the paradoxes but do not confront them before a cultural brand addresses them.

Sometimes cultural brands provide answers to antiglobalization movements. Marc Gobé argued in *Citizen Brand* that ordinary people perceive themselves to be powerless against global companies that show a disregard for both their local communities and the environment.[21] This stimulates an anti-consumerism movement against these global corporations. It also indicates that people are longing for responsible brands that are responsive to consumers and work to make the world a better place. These brands are citizen brands that address the public's interest in good versus bad in their approach to marketing. Cultural brands are sometimes national brands that try to address the preferences of consumers who are against negative global culture, represented by global brands, and who look for alternative brands.[22] Cultural brands play the role of the good guys against global brands—the bad guys. These brands promote nationalism and protectionism because they aim to become the cultural icons for the local society.

Cultural brands tend to be relevant only to certain societies. But this does not mean that global brands cannot be cultural brands. Some well-known global brands are consistently building their cultural brand status. For example, McDonald's positions itself as the icon of globalization. It tries to create the perception that globalization is the symbol of peace and collaboration. It is available to almost everyone in the world. In *The Lexus and the Olive Tree*, Friedman introduced the Golden Arches Theory of Conflict Prevention, which holds that countries with McDonald's restaurants have never gone to war with each other. Later, in *The World Is Flat*, Friedman changed the theory into the Dell Theory of Conflict Prevention, which stated that no countries within Dell's supply chain had gone to war with each other. Instead, they are collaborating to form a supply chain for global society. As a result, Dell is increasingly replacing McDonald's as the icon of globalization.

Another example is The Body Shop, known as a paragon of social equality and justice. Globalization normally does not factor in social justice in its strategy. Globalization applauds the winners in costs and competencies. The strong minority will thrive but the weak majority will strive. This creates a sense of social injustice and became the key theme that The Body Shop is addressing. People perceive that The Body Shop seeks to promote social equality—something that is often neglected in the globalized world. Although sometimes considered anticapitalist or antiglobalization, The Body Shop philosophy is, in fact, in favor of global marketplaces. It believes that justice can only be accomplished through global businesses.

Cultural marketing is the second building block of Marketing 3.0. Marketing 3.0 is an approach that addresses concerns and desires of global citizens. Companies practicing Marketing 3.0 should understand community issues that relates to their business.

Fortunately, the concept of the public's interest is now foreshadowed in the new definition of marketing created by the American Marketing Association in 2008, which reads: "Marketing is the activity, set of institutions, and processes for creating, communicating, delivering, and exchanging offerings that have value for consumers, clients, partners, and society at large."[23] By adding "society," the new definition recognizes that marketing has large-scale impacts beyond what happens in the private dealings of individuals and companies. It also shows that marketing is now ready to address the cultural implications of globalization.

Marketing 3.0 is marketing that puts cultural issues at the heart of a company's business model. In later chapters, we will elaborate on ways a company practicing Marketing 3.0 demonstrates its concern for the communities around it: communities of consumers, employees, channel partners, and shareholders.

THE AGE OF CREATIVE SOCIETY
AND HUMAN SPIRIT MARKETING

The third force that brings forth Marketing 3.0 is the rise of creative society. People in creative society are right-brainers who work in creative sectors such as science, art, and professional services. This type of society, according to Daniel Pink's *A Whole New Mind*, is the highest level of social development in human civilization.[24] Pink portrays human evolution from the primitive hunter, farmer, and blue-collar worker who rely on their muscle and who then evolve into white-collar executives who rely on their left brain and finally progress to artists who rely on their right brain. Technology is once again the primary driver of this evolution.

Research suggests that although the number of creative people is much smaller than the number of working class people, their role in society is increasingly dominant. They are mostly innovators who create and use new technologies and concepts. In the collaborative world influenced by new wave technology, they are the hubs who connect consumers with one another. They are the most expressive and collaborative consumers who make the most use of social media. They influence the overall society with their lifestyles and attitudes. Their opinions toward the globalization paradoxes and issues in the society shape the opinions of others. As the most advanced members of society, they favor collaborative and cultural brands. As pragmatists, they criticize brands that have negative social, economic, and environmental impacts on people's lives.

Around the world, creative society is growing. In *The Rise of the Creative Class*,[25] Richard Florida presents evidence that people in the United States are beginning to work and live like creative scientists and artists. His research reveals that for the past few decades, the investment, output, and workforce in the creative sector in the United States had risen significantly. In *The Flight of the Creative Class*, he describes how he extended his research to other parts of the world and found that European countries also have a high creativity index, which measures creative development of a nation based on its advancement in technology, talent, and tolerance.[26] In advanced nations, creative people are the backbone of the economy. Regions with a cluster of creative people have shown more growth in the past.

Florida's findings do not mean that creativity only belongs to advanced nations. In *The Fortune at the Bottom of the Pyramid*, Prahalad explained how creativity can also sprout in poorer societies. He described several examples of how creativity emerges in response to social issues in rural areas.

Hart and Christensen made similar arguments showing that disruptive innovations often occur among low income markets.[27] Creative low-cost technology often appears in poor countries where the need is to solve problems. India, a place where poverty is a chronic issue, manages to become the world's back office with an abundance of creative technology enthusiasts.

According to Zohar,[28] creativity makes human beings different from other living creatures on earth. Human beings with creativity shape their world. Creative people constantly seek to improve themselves and their world. Creativity expresses itself in humanity, morality, and spirituality.

As the number of creative people increases in developed and developing countries, human civilization is getting closer to its culmination. One of the key characters of an advanced and creative society is that people believe in self-actualization beyond their primal needs for survival. They are expressive and collaborative cocreators. As complex humans, they believe in the human spirit and listen to their deepest desires.

Consider the classic Maslow pyramid depicting the hierarchy of needs. Abraham Maslow showed that humankind has levels of needs that must be met, from survival (basic needs), safety and security, belonging and social, esteem (ego), up to self-actualization (meaning). He also found that the higher needs cannot be met before those below them are met. The pyramid became the root of capitalism. However, in *Spiritual Capital*,[29] Zohar revealed that Maslow, a creative worker himself, before he died regretted what he had said earlier and felt his pyramid ought to have been upside down. The inverted pyramid would then place the fulfillment of self-actualization as a prime need of all human beings.

Creative people are, in fact, strong believers in the inverted Maslow pyramid. The definition of spirituality as "the valuing of the nonmaterial aspects of life and intimations of an enduring reality" really finds its relevance in creative society.[30] Scientists and artists often abandon material fulfillment in pursuit of self-actualization. They seek beyond what money can buy. They search for meaning, happiness, and spiritual realization. Their material fulfillment often comes last as a reward for their achievement. Julia Cameron in *The Artist's Way* elaborates on the life of a creative artist as a unified process of creativity and spirituality.[31] Spirituality and creativity are similar in the mind of an artist. Creativity spurs spirituality. Spiritual need is humanity's greatest motivator, which unleashes deeper personal creativity.

The rise of the creative scientists and artists, consequently, changes the way human beings see their needs and desires. Spirituality is increasingly replacing survival as a prime need of human beings, as observed by Gary Zukav in *The Heart of the Soul*.[32] Nobel Prize-winning economist Robert William Fogel asserted that society today is increasingly in search of spiritual resources on top of material fulfillment.[33]

As a result of this growing trend in society, consumers are now not only looking for products and services that satisfy their needs but also searching for experiences and business models that touch their spiritual side. Supplying meaning is the future value proposition in marketing. The values-driven business model is the new killer app in Marketing 3.0. The findings of Melinda Davis in her Human Desire Project affirm this argument. She found that psychospiritual benefits are indeed the most essential need of consumers and perhaps the ultimate differentiation a marketer can create.[34]

How can companies embed values in their business models? Richard Barrett found that corporations can mount levels of spirituality that resemble those of humans. He found that the human level of spiritual motivation can be adapted into corporate missions, visions, and values.[35] However, we have seen many companies that simply put the values of good corporate citizenship in the mission, vision, and values without really practicing them in business. We have also observed many companies that undertake socially responsible actions as public relations gestures. Marketing 3.0 is not about companies doing public relations. It is about companies weaving values into their corporate cultures.

Like creative people, companies should think about their self-actualization beyond material objectives. They must understand what they are and why they are in business. They should know what they want to become. All these should be in the corporate mission, vision, and values. Profit will result from consumers' appreciation of these companies' contributions to human well-being. This is spiritual or human spirit marketing from a company's point of view. This is the third building block of Marketing 3.0.

MARKETING 3.0: COLLABORATIVE, CULTURAL, AND SPIRITUAL

In summary, the era of Marketing 3.0 is the era where marketing practices are very much influenced by changes in consumer behavior and attitude. It is the more sophisticated form of the consumer-centric era where the consumer demands more collaborative, cultural, and spiritual marketing approaches. (See Figure 1.1.)

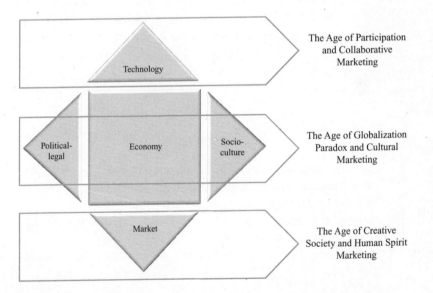

Figure 1.1 Three Changes that Lead to Marketing 3.0

Table 1.2 Building Blocks of Marketing 3.0

Building Blocks		Why?
What to Offer		
Content	Collaborative Marketing	The Age of Participation (the Stimulus)
Context	Cultural Marketing	The Age of Globalization Paradox (the Problem)
How to Offer	Spiritual Marketing	The Age of Creativity (the Solution)

New wave technology facilitates the widespread dissemination of information, ideas, and public opinion that enable consumers to collaborate for value creation. Technology drives globalization of the political and legal, economy, and social culture landscape, which creates cultural paradoxes in the society. Technology also drives the rise of the creative market, which is more spiritual in viewing the world.

As consumers become more collaborative, cultural, and spiritual, the character of marketing also transforms. Table 1.2 summarizes the three building blocks of Marketing 3.0. In the next chapters, we will elaborate on Marketing 3.0 in greater detail including how to apply it to various communities of stakeholders and how to translate it into a company's business model.

NOTES

1. The term *new wave technology* was inspired by the term *fifth-wave computing* in Michael V. Copeland and Om Malik, "How to Ride the Fifth Wave," *Business 2.0*, July 2005.
2. Stephen Baker and Heather Green, "Social Media Will Change Your Business," *BusinessWeek*, February 20, 2008.
3. Rick Murray, *A Corporate Guide to the Global Blogosphere: The New Model of Peer-to-Peer Communications*, Edelman, 2007.
4. Steven Johnson, "How Twitter Will Change the Way We Live," *Time*, June 15, 2009.

5. Stephen Baker, "What's A Friend Worth?" *BusinessWeek*, June 1, 2009.
6. From the website <wikipedia.org>, accessed in June 2009.
7. "Mass collaboration could change way companies operate," *USA Today*, December 26, 2006.
8. Henry Chesbrough, *Open Business Models: How to Thrive in the New Innovation Landscape* (Harvard Business School Press, 2006).
9. Don Tapscott and Anthony D. Williams, *Wikinomics: How Mass Collaboration Changes Everything* (New York: Portfolio, 2006).
10. Alex Wipperfürth, *Brand Hijack: Marketing without Marketing* (New York: Portfolio, 2005).
11. *Consumer-made*, www.trendwatching.com/trends/consumer-made.htm.
12. Ori Brafman and Rod A. Beckstrom, *The Starfish and the Spider: The Unstoppable Power of Leaderless Organizations* (New York: Portfolio, 2006).
13. Larry Huston and Nabil Sakkab, "Connect and Develop: Inside Procter & Gamble's New Model for Innovation," *Harvard Business Review*, March 2006.
14. C.K. Prahalad and Venkat Ramaswamy, *The Future of Competition: Co-creating Unique Value with Consumers* (Boston: Harvard Business School Press, 2004).
15. Thomas L. Friedman, *The World is Flat: A Brief History of the Globalized World in the 21st Century* (London: Penguin Group, 2005).
16. Robert J. Samuelson, "The World Is Still Round," *Newsweek*, July 25, 2005.
17. Benjamin Barber, *Jihad vs. McWorld: How Globalism and Tribalism Are Reshaping the World* (New York: Ballantine Books, 1996).
18. Thomas Friedman, *The Lexus and the Olive Tree: Understanding Globalization* (New York: Anchor Books, 2000).
19. Charles Handy, *The Age of Paradox* (Boston: Harvard Business School Press, 1994).
20. Douglas B. Holt, *How Brands Become Icons: The Principles of Cultural Branding* (Boston: Harvard Business School Press, 2004).
21. Marc Gobé, *Citizen Brand: 10 Commandments for Transforming Brand Culture in a Consumer Democracy* (New York: Allworth Press, 2002).

22. Paul A. Laudicina, *World Out of Balance: Navigating Global Risks to Seize Competitive Advantage* (New York: McGraw-Hill, 2005).

23. "The American Marketing Association Releases New Definition for Marketing," Press Release, American Marketing Association, January 14, 2008.

24. Daniel H. Pink, *A Whole New Mind: Moving from the Information Age to the Conceptual Age* (New York: Riverhead Books, 2005).

25. Richard Florida, *The Rise of Creative Class: And How It's Transforming Work, Leisure, Community and Everyday Life* (New York: Basic Books, 2002).

26. Richard Florida, *The Flight of the Creative Class: The New Global Competition for Talent* (New York: HarperBusiness, 2005).

27. Stuart L. Hart and Clayton M. Christensen, "The Great Leap: Driving Innovation from the Base of the Pyramid," *MIT Sloan Management Review*, October 15, 2002.

28. Danah Zohar, *The Quantum Self: Human Nature and Consciousness Defined by the New Physics* (New York: Quill, 1990).

29. Danah Zohar and Ian Marshall, *Spiritual Capital: Wealth We Can Live By* (San Francisco: Berrett-Koehler Publishers, 2004).

30. The definition of spirituality is cited from Charles Handy, *The Hungry Spirit: Beyond Capitalism, A Quest for Purpose in the Modern World* (New York: Broadway Books, 1998).

31. Julia Cameron, *The Artist's Way: A Spiritual Path to Higher Creativity* (New York: Tarcher, 1992).

32. Gary Zukav, *The Heart of Soul: Emotional Awareness* (New York: Free Press, 2002).

33. Robert William Fogel, *The Fourth Awakening and the Future of Egalitarianism* (Chicago: University of Chicago Press, 2000).

34. Melinda Davis, *The New Culture of Desire: Five Radical New Strategies that Will Change Your Business and Your Life* (New York: Free Press, 2002).

35. Richard Barrett, *Liberating the Corporate Soul: Building a Visionary Organization* (Butterworth-Heinemann, 1998).

CHAPTER TWO

Future Model for Marketing 3.0

THE PAST 60 YEARS OF MARKETING: A BRIEF RETROSPECT

Marketing has been one of the most exciting subjects in the business world during the past six decades. In a nutshell, marketing has revolved around three major disciplines: *product management*, *customer management*, and *brand management*. In fact, marketing concepts evolved from a focus on product management in the 1950s and 1960s to a focus on customer management in the 1970s and the 1980s. It then evolved further and added the discipline of brand management in the 1990s and the 2000s. The continuous adaptation of marketing concepts to different eras of human lives is what keeps it exciting.

Ever since Neil Borden coined the infamous "marketing-mix" term in the 1950s and Jerome McCarthy introduced the four Ps in the 1960s, marketing concepts have undergone significant transformation while adapting to the changing environment.[1] The manufacturing sector was the center of the U.S. economy in the postwar 1950s and continued to soar during the 1960s. In such an environment, it was logical

25

to see the development of marketing concepts simply focused on the product management discipline.

Marketing was initially viewed as just one of several important functions supporting production, along with finance and human resources. The key function of marketing was to generate demand for products. McCarthy's four Ps concisely explained the generic practices of product management in those days: develop a *product*, determine the *price*, do the *promotion*, and set up the *place* of distribution. As business was on the upswing during those two decades, nothing more was needed from marketing other than those tactical guidelines.

It all suddenly changed when the U.S. economy—and the Western economy in general—was hit by oil shock-driven stagflation in the 1970s. The economy remained uncertain throughout the 1980s because economic growth had mostly migrated to developing countries in Asia. Generating demand during these turbulent and uncertain times was harder and required more than just the four Ps. Demand was scarce. Some products were launched to compete with one another to win buyers. Over the course of these two decades, consumers became smarter buyers. In consumers' minds, many products were seen as commodities because they had no distinct positioning. The changing environment forced marketing professionals to think harder and create better concepts.

More Ps—people, process, physical evidence, public opinion, and political power—joined the original four Ps.[2] However, the classic model of Marketing 1.0 remained tactical in nature. Perhaps the downswing was a blessing in disguise, as marketing finally gained prominence during this period of low demand. To stimulate demand for products, marketing evolved from a purely tactical to a more strategic level. Marketers realized that to effectively generate demand, "customer" should replace "product" at the heart of all marketing activities. The customer management discipline, including strategies such as segmentation, targeting, and positioning (STP), was introduced. At this point, marketing was no longer only tactical. As it focused more on the customers than on the products, marketing became strategic. Since then, the development of the four Ps has always been preceded by the development of the STP. The introduction of the strategic marketing model marked the birth of modern marketing. This was the origin of Marketing 2.0.

In Chapter 1, we argued that 1989 was the tipping point for globalization. Many paradoxical events occurred in that particular year. The year 1989 proved to be the tipping point for marketing as well. The personal computer had entered the mainstream and the Internet was born as a strong complement in the early 1990s. The networking of computers was accompanied by the networking of humans. Network computing enabled more human-to-human interaction and facilitated the spread of word-of-mouth information sharing. It made information ubiquitous and no longer scarce. Consumers became well connected and thus well informed.

To embrace these changes, marketers around the world expanded the concept of marketing to focus on human emotions. They introduced new concepts such as emotional marketing, experiential marketing, and brand equity. To generate demand, it was no longer enough to target the customer's mind with the classic positioning model. It was necessary to target the customer's heart as well. The marketing concepts that emerged in the 1990s and the 2000s mostly reflected the brand management discipline.

Looking back, we can see that the marketing discipline passed through several stages with an exploding number of new concepts. Figure 2.1 shows the main concepts that appeared in each of the decades since the 1950s. Clearly the dynamism of marketing and its practitioners' ceaseless determination to develop new ways to understand the changing markets, customers, competitors, and collaborators gave birth to new understandings and tools.

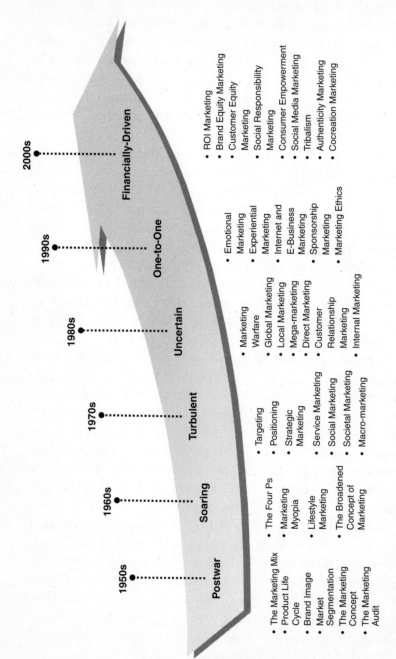

Figure 2.1 The Evolution of Marketing Concepts

THE FUTURE OF MARKETING:
HORIZONTAL NOT VERTICAL

The future of marketing will be partly shaped by current developments and partly by long run forces. In recent years, companies around the world have experienced the deepest recession since the Great Depression of the 1930s. The major fault was overly loose credit extended in the form of mortgages, credit cards, and commercial and residential loans to persons and organizations that could not repay their debts. The culprits were banks, greedy investors, speculators, and junk bond dealers. When the financial bubble burst and housing values nosedived, both the poor and the rich became poorer. Customers cut their spending and shifted their spending to cheaper brands and products. This was disastrous for the U.S. economy where 70 percent of the GDP was made up of consumer spending. Companies laid off many of their workers and unemployment rose from 5 to 10 percent.

The new Obama administration immediately arranged for billions of stimulus dollars to help prop up the economy. It wanted to avoid more corporate implosions like the ones that destroyed Bears Stearns and Lehman Brothers and nearly wiped out AIG, General Motors, and others. The stimulus came just in time and stabilized the situation in mid-2009 without promising much of a recovery; at best, it promised a very slow recovery.

The question is whether consumers in the new decade beginning in 2010 will spend more cautiously than they did in the past. The preceding lifestyle of "buy now, pay later" is less likely to reoccur, partly because of government plans to regulate credit more tightly and partly because of consumer fears and risk aversion. Consumers may want to save more for another rainy day. If spending remains low, then economic growth will be slow, each reinforcing the other. This means that marketers will have to work harder than ever to separate consumers from their dollars.

Marketing 1.0 and 2.0 will still have some relevance. Marketing is still about developing segmentation, choosing the target segment, defining the positioning, providing the four Ps, and building brand around the product. However, the changes in the business environment—recession, climate concerns, new social media, consumer empowerment, new wave technology, and globalization—will continue to create a massive shift in marketing practices.

New marketing concepts always emerge as a reaction to the changing business environment. A recent McKinsey & Company research report lists 10 trends in business following the financial crisis of 2007–2009.[3] One major trend reveals that the market in which businesses operate is increasingly turning into a low-trust environment. The Chicago Booth/Kellogg School Financial Trust Index shows that most Americans have the least trust toward large corporations in which they can invest their money. The vertical distrust goes both ways. Financial institutions have also stopped giving credit to consumers.

Today, trust exists more in horizontal relationships than in vertical relationships. Consumers believe one another more than they believe in companies. The rise of social media is simply a reflection of the migration of consumers' trusts from companies to other consumers. According to Nielsen Global Survey, fewer consumers rely on company-generated advertising.[4] Consumers turn to word of mouth as a new and credible form of advertising they can trust. Around 90 percent of consumers surveyed trust recommendations from people they know. Moreover, 70 percent of consumers believe in customer opinions posted online. The research by Trendstream/Lightspeed Research interestingly shows that consumers trust strangers in their social network more than they trust experts.

All these research findings serve as an early warning for corporations that consumers in general have lost their faith in business practices. Some may argue that this is a business ethics issue and way beyond the reach of marketers.

Unfortunately, marketing is partly responsible for this. Marketing is considered the same as selling, using the art of persuasion, and even some manipulation. Even after the birth of modern marketing, which aims to serve consumers, marketing often continues to make exaggerated claims about product performance and differentiation in order to make a sale.

Read the following anecdote about Exxon Mobil a few decades ago—now a company that topped the 2009 Fortune 500 list.

> Back in the early 1980s, Exxon Oil Co. held an employee conference to announce its new "core values." Number one on the list was the simple statement, "The customer comes first." That evening, division executives discussed the values statement over dinner. One brash young rising star, a fellow named Monty, proposed a toast. "I just want you to know," he began, "that the customer does not come first." Monty pointed at the president of the division. "He comes first." He named the European president. "He comes second." He named the North American president. "He comes third." Monty rattled off four more senior executives of the division, all of whom were in the room. "The customer," he concluded, "comes eighth." A stunned silence overtook the room before one of the executives smiled, and the gathered group burst out into hysterical laughter. It was the first truth spoken all day.[5]

It happened a long time ago but we can easily find similar stories today. Many marketers should confess that deep in their hearts consumers are never their top priority. Marketing may be responsible for the decline in consumers' trust but it also has the biggest chance to solve this issue. After all, marketing is the managerial process that is the closest to the consumers.

We believe it is time to put an end to the marketer-consumer dichotomy. Marketers of any product or service should realize that they are also consumers of other products and services. Consumers should also be aware that they might practice marketing as well in their daily lives to

Table 2.1   The Future of Marketing

The Disciplines of Marketing	Today's Marketing Concept	Future Marketing Concept
Product Management	The Four Ps (product, price, place, promotion)	Cocreation
Customer Management	STP (segmentation, targeting, and positioning)	Communitization
Brand Management	Brand building	Character building

convince their fellow consumers. Everyone is both marketer and consumer. Marketing is not just something marketers do to consumers. Consumers are marketing to other consumers as well.

We see that marketing concepts over the past 60 years are mostly vertical. To regain the consumers' trust is to embrace what we call "the new consumer trust system." The new consumer trust system is horizontal. Consumers today gather in their own communities, cocreate their own products and experiences, and only look outside of their community for admirable characters. They are skeptical because they know that good characters are scarce outside their communities. But once they find one, they will instantly be loyal evangelists.

To succeed, companies should understand that consumers increasingly appreciate cocreation, communitization, and characters (see Table 2.1). Let us examine these three things that we predict will be the three cornerstones of future marketing practices.

Cocreation

Cocreation is a term coined by C.K. Prahalad that describes the new approach to innovation. Prahalad and Krishnan in *The New Age of Innovation* observed the new ways of creating product and experience through collaboration by companies, consumers, suppliers, and channel partners interconnected in a network of innovation.[6] A product experience is never a product experience by itself. It is the accumulation of individual consumer experiences that creates the most value for the product. When individual consumers experience the product, they personalize the experience according to their own unique needs and wants.

We observe three key processes of cocreation. First, companies should create what we call a "platform," which is a generic product that can be customized further. Secondly, let individual consumers within a network customize the platform to match their own unique identities. Finally, ask for consumer feedback and enrich the platform by incorporating all the customization efforts made by the network of consumers. This practice is common in the open source approach of software development and we believe its application can be stretched to other industries as well. This is how companies should take advantage of the cocreation happening in the consumers' horizontal network.

Communitization

Technology not only connects and propels countries and companies toward globalization but also connects and propels consumers toward communitization. The concept of communitization is closely related to the concept of tribalism in marketing. In *Tribes*, Seth Godin argued that consumers want to be connected to other consumers not to companies.[7] Companies that want to embrace this new trend should accommodate this need and help consumers connect to one another in communities. Godin argued that succeeding in business requires the support of communities.

According to Fournier and Lee, consumers can organize into communities of *pools, webs,* or *hubs*.[8] Consumers in pools share the same values although they do not necessarily interact with one another. The only thing keeping them together is their belief and strong affiliation to a brand. This type of community is a typical group of brand enthusiasts that many companies should nurture. Consumers in webs, on the other hand, interact with one another. This is a typical social media community where the bond is rooted in one-to-one relationships among the members. Consumers in hubs are different. They gravitate around a strong figure and create a loyal fan base. The classification of community is consistent with Godin's argument that consumers are either connected to one another (webs), to a leader (hubs), or to an idea (pools). Godin, Fournier, and Lee all agree that communities exist not to serve the business but to service the members. Companies should be aware of this and participate in serving the members of the communities.

Character Building

For brands to be able to connect with human beings, brands need to develop an authentic DNA that is the core of their true differentiation. This DNA will reflect the brand's identity in consumers' social networks. Brands with unique DNAs will have their characters built up throughout their lives. Achieving differentiation is already hard for marketers. Achieving authentic differentiation is even harder.

In their new book, *Authenticity*,[9] Pine and Gilmore argue that when today's consumers view a brand, they can and will immediately judge whether it is fake or real. Companies should always try to be real and deliver experiences that live up to what they claim. They should not try to only appear real in the advertising or they will instantly lose credibility. In the horizontal world of consumers, losing credibility means losing the whole network of potential buyers.

SHIFT TO HUMAN SPIRIT: THE 3i MODEL

In Marketing 3.0, companies need to address consumers as whole human beings. According to Stephen Covey, a whole human has four basic components: a physical body, a mind capable of independent thought and analysis, a heart that can feel emotion, and a spirit—your soul or philosophical center.[10]

In marketing, the concept of being relevant to the consumer's mind began with Al Ries and Jack Trout's classic book *Positioning*.[11] They argued that the idea of the product must be positioned meaningfully and uniquely in the mind of the target customers. Thus, the marketers of the Volvo automobile were extremely successful in planting the idea in the mind of automobile buyers that Volvo offered the most safety of any car.

But later, we began to recognize that the emotional component of the human psyche was being neglected. Targeting the mind is no longer enough. Marketers should also target the hearts of consumers. The concept of emotional marketing has been described in several books such as *Experiential Marketing* by Bernd Schmitt, *Emotional Branding* by Marc Gobé, and *Lovemarks* by Kevin Roberts, to name a few.[12]

Great examples of emotional marketing were achieved by marketers such as Howard Schultz of Starbucks, Richard Branson of Virgin, and Steve Jobs of Apple. Starbucks' concept of "third place for drinking coffee," Virgin's "unconventional marketing," and Apple's "creative imagination" are the implementations of emotionally relevant marketing. These efforts were aimed at our emotional hearts, which bear our feelings.

Marketing will need to evolve to a third stage where it addresses the spirit of the consumers. Marketers should try to understand the anxieties and desires of the consumers and do what Stephen Covey calls "unlock the soul's code" in order to stay relevant. Companies should target consumers as whole human beings who consist of minds, hearts, and spirits. The point is not to overlook the spirit.

In 3.0, marketing should be redefined as a consonant triangle of brand, positioning, and differentiation.[13] To complete the triangle, we introduce the 3i: brand *identity*, brand *integrity*, and brand *image*. In the horizontal world of consumers, brand is useless if it only articulates its positioning.

Figure 2.2 The 3i Model

The brand may have a clear identity in consumers' minds but not necessarily a good one. Positioning is a mere claim that alerts consumers to be cautious of an inauthentic brand. In other words, the triangle is not complete without the differentiation. Differentiation is the brand's DNA that reflects the true integrity of the brand. It is a solid proof that a brand is delivering what it promises. It is essentially about delivering the promised performance and satisfaction to your customers. Differentiation that is synergetic to the positioning will automatically create a good brand image. Only a complete triangle is a credible one in Marketing 3.0 (see Figure 2.2).

Brand identity is about positioning your brand in the minds of the consumers. The positioning should be unique for your brand to be heard and noticed in the cluttered marketplace. It should also be relevant to the rational needs and wants of the consumers. On the other hand, brand integrity is about fulfilling what is claimed through the positioning and differentiation of the brand. It is about being credible, fulfilling your promise, and establishing consumers' trust in your brand. The target of brand integrity is the spirit of the consumers. Finally, brand image is about acquiring a strong share of the consumer's emotions. Your brand value should appeal to consumers' emotional needs and wants beyond product functionalities and features. You can see that the triangle is intended to be relevant to whole human beings with minds, hearts, and spirits.

Another essential takeaway from this model is that in Marketing 3.0, marketers should target consumers' minds and spirits simultaneously to touch their hearts. Positioning will trigger the mind to consider a buying decision. A brand requires an authentic differentiation for the human spirit to confirm the decision. Finally, the heart will lead a consumer to act and make the buying decision.

For example, S.C. Johnson & Son, Inc., positioned itself as "the sustainable five-generation family company that specializes in home care consumer products." The differentiation lies in the sustainable business model. The term "bottom of the pyramid"—referring to people earning less than $1 a day—has been very popular since C.K. Prahalad wrote *Fortune at the Bottom of the Pyramid*, a book about serving the poor as a profitable and sustainable business.[14] However, it was S.C. Johnson & Son that pioneered the practice of serving the bottom of the pyramid in various markets such as Kenya. For the last few years, S.C. Johnson & Son has been a key partner in the development of the bottom of the pyramid protocol with Stuart L. Hart, author of *Capitalism at the Crossroads*. Therefore, the corporate brand has the integrity to be positioned as the sustainable five-generation family company (see Figure 2.3).

Timberland is another good example of a company with a solid brand integrity. It is positioned as "the good outdoor-inspired footwear and apparel company" (Figure 2.4). The company supports its positioning with a solid differentiation. It is well-known for its "Path of Service," the community volunteer service program that involves employees of Timberland. The differentiation is already proven since it stands the test of

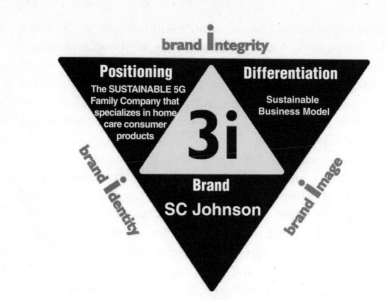

Figure 2.3   The 3i of S.C. Johnson

Figure 2.4   The 3i of Timberland

time. In 1994, the company's net profits fell from $22.5 million to $17.7 million. The following year, sales stayed stagnant, and the company posted an earnings loss for the very first time. Many people predicted that the Path of Service program would be eliminated under such circumstances. But Timberland's leaders believed that community volunteer service is an integral part of the corporate DNA that makes the brand different and authentic. Therefore, the program continues to this day.[15]

The 3i model is also very relevant for marketing in the context of social media. In the era of consumer empowerment led by abundant information and networked communities, a consonant brand-positioning-differentiation is all you need. There is no chance for inauthentic brands to survive when word-of-mouth becomes the new advertising medium and consumers believe strangers within their community more than they believe companies. Lies and hoaxes exist in social media but they will be exposed quickly by the collective wisdom of the community of consumers.

In social media, a brand is like a member. The brand identity (that is, your avatar) is rated by accumulation of experience within the community. One bad experience will spoil your brand integrity and destroy your brand image in the community. Every social media user knows this. Social media elites guard their characters relentlessly. Marketers should beware of and embrace this trend. Do not enforce too much control over the community of consumers and let them do the marketing for you. Just be true to your brand DNA. Marketing 3.0 is the era of horizontal communication where vertical control will not work. Only honesty, originality, and authenticity will.

SHIFT TO VALUES-DRIVEN MARKETING

Marketers need to identify the anxieties and desires of the consumers to be able to target their minds, hearts, and spirits. In the globalization paradox, the generic anxiety and desire of the consumers is to make their society—and the world at large—a better, perhaps even an ideal place to live. Therefore, companies that intend to be icons should share the same dream with consumers and make a difference.

Some companies are making a difference by means of corporate philanthropy for a social or environmental cause. According to the book *Compassionate Capitalism*, corporate philanthropy is a great way for companies to start building a good business.[16] First, it makes the corporate leaders passionate about a social cause and therefore encourages them to donate personal and/or corporate money to it. Second, the company starts to realize that corporate philanthropy has marketing value. However, these two starting points very often fail. Companies that take the first approach usually fail to incorporate philanthropy as part of the corporate DNA. The ones that take the second approach usually have difficulty in maintaining commitment. Many companies would have difficulty justifying what Timberland did when it maintained the volunteer program during tough times. Moreover, companies can fall into a trap of being inauthentic—doing good activities just to make a sale.

Mission, Vision, and Values

To include good deeds in a corporate culture and maintain commitment, the best approach is to embed them into the company's mission, vision, and values. Corporate leaders need to think about these statements as the corporate DNA. Look at the inspiring story of Fetzer Vineyards under the leadership of Paul Dolan.[17] Dolan realized that to make Fetzer Vineyards an admirable company that demonstrates the best practice of sustainability as well as a proud member of the community, the commitment needs to start at the corporate level, so that all employees take it seriously.

The late Peter Drucker also once argued that starting with a mission may be the first lesson business can learn from successful nonprofits.[18] Drucker argued that successful businesses do not start their planning with financial returns. They start with the performance of their mission. Financial returns will come as results.

Some people define mission as a statement that expresses the business your company is in. In a dynamic business environment, the definition of business scope can change very fluidly. Therefore, we prefer to define a mission in more enduring terms as your company's reason for being; it reflects the company's basic purpose for existence. A company should characterize its mission as fundamentally as possible, as it will determine the sustainability of the company.

Inspired by a famous principle of Charles Handy, we symbolize a company's mission with a doughnut.[19] The doughnut principle basically says that life is like an inverted doughnut, in which the hole is on the outside and the dough is in the middle. In the doughnut view of life, the core is fixed and the bounded space around the core is flexible. The company's mission is the core that cannot be changed. The operations and business scope of the company are flexible but should be aligned with the core.

While mission is firmly rooted in the past when the company was established, vision is about inventing the future. Vision can be defined as a picture of the desirable future state of the company. It explains what the company aspires to become and achieve. To define this, a company needs to create a mental picture of the future given the definition of the corporate mission. We symbolize it by a compass that guides a company to its future state.

On the other hand, values can be considered as "a corporation's institutional standards of behavior."[20] Because companies generally follow the same values cycle, they are symbolized as a wheel. Values articulate a set of corporate priorities and management attempts to embed them in its practices, which it hopes will reinforce behaviors that benefit the company and communities inside and outside the firm, and which in turn strengthen the institution's values.

In summary, a values-based matrix should also be introduced where, on one axis, the company strives to occupy

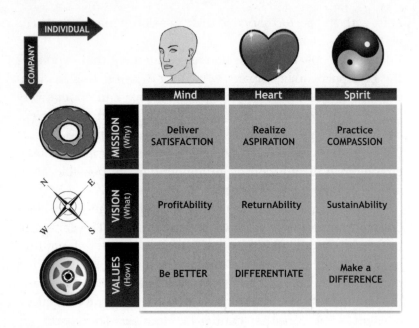

Figure 2.5   Values-Based Matrix (VBM) Model

the minds, hearts, and spirits of current and future customers. The other axis takes into account the company's mission, vision, and values (Figure 2.5). While delivering performance and satisfaction to the customers at the product level is essential, at the highest level, a brand ought to be seen as realizing emotional aspirations and practicing compassion in some form. It must not only promise ProfitAbility and ReturnAbility to current and future shareholders, but also SustainAbility. It must also become a brand that is better, different, and that makes a difference to current and future employees.

For example, S.C. Johnson & Son embeds its commitment to social and environmental sustainability in the mission, vision, and values of the company (Figure 2.6). With the mission of "contributing to the community well-being as well as sustaining and protecting the environment," S.C. Johnson & Son

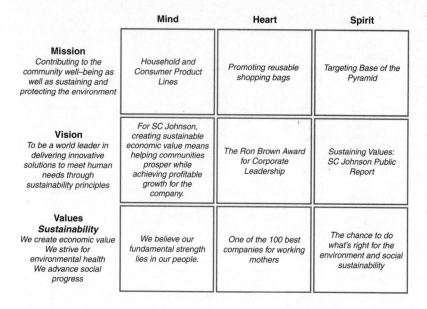

	Mind	Heart	Spirit
Mission *Contributing to the community well–being as well as sustaining and protecting the environment*	*Household and Consumer Product Lines*	*Promoting reusable shopping bags*	*Targeting Base of the Pyramid*
Vision *To be a world leader in delivering innovative solutions to meet human needs through sustainability principles*	*For SC Johnson, creating sustainable economic value means helping communities prosper while achieving profitable growth for the company.*	*The Ron Brown Award for Corporate Leadership*	*Sustaining Values: SC Johnson Public Report*
Values **Sustainability** *We create economic value We strive for environmental health We advance social progress*	*We believe our fundamental strength lies in our people.*	*One of the 100 best companies for working mothers*	*The chance to do what's right for the environment and social sustainability*

Figure 2.6 Values-Based Matrix of S.C. Johnson

satisfies consumers by providing various products, realizes aspirations by inviting customer participation in sustaining the environment, and practices compassion by targeting the base of the pyramid market.

The company has the vision to be the world leader in delivering innovative solutions to meet human needs through sustainable principles. The achievement of the vision is marked by profitable growth and several awards presented to the company. It also releases a public report to share its achievement in the area of sustainability.

The values of S.C. Johnson & Son are rooted in the concept of the triple bottom line: economic value, environmental health, and social progress. To target the minds, hearts, and spirit of current and future employees, the company uses the triple bottom line concept. By saying that the company's fundamental strength lies in its people, it targets the mind. To target the heart, the company hires mothers and was dubbed

	Mind	**Heart**	**Spirit**
Mission *Make it better*	*High quality products*	*Outdoor store design*	*Tagline: "Make it Better"*
Vision *To be a twenty-first century example for socially-responsible corporations around the world*	*Profit growth*	*Stock performance*	*Sustainability Key Performance Indicators*
Values *Humanity* *Humility* *Integrity* *Excellence*	*"At our corporate headquarters, employees work hard to make some of the world's most innovative products"*	*Fortune 100 Best Companies to Work For*	*Path of Service*

Figure 2.7   Values-Based Matrix of Timberland

one of the 100 best companies for working mothers. By offering the opportunity to do what's right for the environment and social sustainability, the company targets the spirit.

Consider the Timberland example. Timberland has a simple mission of making its products better (Figure 2.7). It delivers customer satisfaction through its quality products and fosters emotional experiences through store design, for example. To target the spirit, it includes the mission as a tagline.

Timberland has the vision to be the twenty-first-century example of a socially responsible corporation around the world. It shows a remarkable achievement for its vision over the past years and can use the achievement to market the company to shareholders. Rationally, the vision is shown by the profit growth the company is enjoying. Emotionally, it is shown by the impressive stock performance. Spiritually, it is shown by the Sustainability Key Performance Indicators.

For its employees, Timberland builds the values of humanity, humility, integrity, and excellence. It demonstrates these values to the employees through various efforts. The most important one is the Path of Service, which provides the opportunity for employees to practice the values.

MARKETING 3.0: THE MEANING OF MARKETING AND THE MARKETING OF MEANING

By closely examining the 3i model you will see the new meaning of marketing in 3.0. Marketing in its culmination will be a consonance of three concepts: identity, integrity, and image. Marketing is about clearly defining your unique identity and strengthening it with authentic integrity to build a strong image.

Marketing 3.0 is also about the marketing of meaning embedded in the corporate mission, vision, and values. By defining marketing in this manner, we wish to elevate the state of marketing further into being a major player in the designing of the company's strategic future. Marketing should no longer be considered as only selling and using tools to generate demand. Marketing should now be considered as the major hope of a company to restore consumer trust.

NOTES

1. Neil Borden mentioned the term "marketing mix" in 1953 in his American Marketing Association presidential address. The four Ps were later introduced in Jerome McCarthy's *Basic Marketing: A Managerial Approach* (1st edition) (Homewood, IL: Irwin, 1960).
2. Public opinion and political power were added by Kotler in 1984; people, process, and physical evidence were added by Boom and Bitner in 1981.
3. Eric Beinhocker, Ian Davis, and Lenny Mendonca, "The Ten Trends You Have to Watch," *Harvard Business Review*, July–August 2009.
4. "Personal Recommendations and Consumer Opinions Posted Online Are the Most Trusted Forms of Advertising Globally," press release (New York: The Nielsen Company, July 7, 2009).

5. Art Kleiner, *Who Really Matters: The Core Group Theory of Power, Privilege, and Success* (New York: The Doubleday Broadway Publishing Group, 2003).

6. C.K. Prahalad and M.S. Krishnan, *The New Age of Innovation: Driving Co-created Value through Global Networks* (New York: McGraw-Hill, 2008).

7. Seth Godin, *Tribes: We Need You to Lead Us* (New York: Portfolio, 2008).

8. Susan Fournier and Lara Lee, "Getting Brand Communities Right," *Harvard Business Review*, April 2009.

9. James H. Gilmore and B. Joseph Pine II, *Authenticity: What Consumers Really Want* (Boston: Harvard Business School Press, 2007).

10. Stephen R. Covey, *The 8th Habit: From Effectiveness to Greatness* (New York: Free Press, 2004).

11. Al Ries and Jack Trout, *Positioning: The Battle for Your Mind* (New York: McGraw-Hill, 1981).

12. For further reading, see Bernd H. Schmitt, *Experiential Marketing: How to Get Customers to Sense, Think, Act, Relate to Your Company and Brands* (New York: Free Press, 1999); Marc Gobé, *Emotional Branding: The New Paradigm for Connecting Brands to People* (New York: Allworth Press, 2001); Kevin Roberts, *Lovemarks: The Future Beyond Brands* (New York: Powerhouse Books, 2004).

13. The original Brand-Positioning-Differentiation Triangle can be found in Philip Kotler, Hermawan Kartajaya, Hooi Den Huan, and Sandra Liu, *Rethinking Marketing: Sustainable Marketing Enterprise in Asia* (Singapore: Pearson Education Asia, 2002).

14. C.K. Prahalad, *The Fortune at the Bottom of the Pyramid: Eradicating Poverty through Profits* (Philadelphia: Wharton School Publishing, 2005).

15. James Austin, Herman B. Leonard, and James W. Quinn, "Timberland: Commerce and Justice," Harvard Business School Case, revised December 21, 2004.

16. Marc Benioff and Karen Southwick, *Compassionate Capitalism: How Corporations Can Make Doing Good an Integral Part of Doing Well* (Franklin Lakes, New Jersey: The Career Press Inc., 2004).

17. Paul Dolan and Thom Elkjer, *True to Our Roots: Fermenting a Business Revolution* (New York: Bloomberg Press, 2003).

18. Peter F. Drucker, "What Business Can Learn from Nonprofits," *Classic Drucker* (Boston: Harvard Business School Press, 2006).

19. Charles Handy, "Finding Sense in Uncertainty" in Rowan Gibson, *Rethinking the Future: Rethinking Business, Principles, Competition, Control and Complexity, Leadership, Markets, and the World* (London: Nicholas Brealey Publishing, 1997).

20. Reggie Van Lee, Lisa Fabish, and Nancy McGaw, "The Value of Corporate Values," *strategy+business*, Issue 39.

PART II

STRATEGY

CHAPTER THREE

Marketing the Mission to the Consumers

CONSUMERS ARE THE NEW BRAND OWNERS!

Remember 1985's New Coke story? In less than three months, New Coke was withdrawn from the market due to consumer backlash.[1] The backlash was not at all about the new taste. In the mid-1980s, Coca-Cola was already part of the pop culture in the United States. Consumers felt a bond with the brand and its infamous secret formula. The New Coke ruined the bond and thus, consumers rejected the new product launch. In Canada, it was a different case. New Coke was well-accepted because Coca-Cola did not have iconic status there. In the United States, it was a costly flop but Coca-Cola could by then be sure that consumers were guarding the brand.

In the contemporary world of the twenty-first century, the scene repeated. This time, it happened to IKEA, the affordable Scandinavian-design furniture retailer. In 2009, in a cost-saving move, IKEA changed the official font from the stylish custom-Futura to the functional Verdana.[2] Consumers reacted with outrage and the conversation spread widely on Twitter. Again, consumers tried to guard the brand they had bonded with. Social media helped in spreading the complaints faster and wider.

When the New Coke case happened, many marketing pundits believed that it was a case of product development failure. The Coca-Cola management simply misinterpreted market research findings and therefore misunderstood consumers' needs and wants. However, when a similar situation happened with IKEA, we can see that such backlashes are more than just launch failures. When a brand's mission is successfully implanted in consumers' minds, hearts, and spirits, the brand is owned by the consumers. The real mistake both companies made was that they did not understand their own brand mission as well as their consumers did.

Coca-Cola is a symbol of American happiness. The brand popularized the happy portrayal of Santa Claus in the 1930s. The 1971 song "I'd Like to Teach the World to Sing" taught Americans to be happy in turbulent times. The mystery surrounding the original formula was considered the secret of happiness. Coca-Cola later launched the "Open Happiness" campaign in 2009, but in the 1980s it was a well-guarded secret. Coca-Cola was even withdrawn from India in 1977 to guard the secret from the Indian government. For Coca-Cola, New Coke was about creating a new taste to win the cola war against Pepsi. But for consumers, it tampered with the secret behind the icon of their happiness. Good news for Coca-Cola: their consumers strongly believed in the brand mission of happiness.

IKEA, too, is an icon. It is a symbol of a smart, stylish lifestyle. Before IKEA, affordable furniture meant functional furniture with no touch of style. IKEA changed all that. For IKEA, affordability means self-service and self-assemble furniture but with great design. The IKEA brand mission: making stylish furniture affordable for smart consumers. The change to the Verdana font might have improved affordability, but it killed the stylish design factor. Altogether, it was not a good move, especially for consumers who adore the righteous brand mission so much. For IKEA, it was a significant cost savings considering the ubiquity of the Verdana font. For consumers, it was a betrayal of their beliefs and knocked off the idea that they are really smart buyers. Again, business consideration was misaligned with the brand mission.

These two cases serve as examples of a very important message: in Marketing 3.0, you don't really own your brands once they are successful. Companies embracing Marketing 3.0 have to live with the fact that exerting control over the brand is almost impossible. The brands belong to their consumers. The brand mission is now their mission. What companies can do is align their actions with the brand mission.

GOOD MISSION DEFINED

Brand mission is not as easy as it seems to craft. It is difficult to summarize why your brand should exist in one simple statement, especially if you want it to be both groundbreaking and not wishy-washy. If you have difficulty stating your brand mission, you are not alone. Jack and Suzy Welch conducted an annual two-day seminar for three consecutive years with about 100 CEOs. To their surprise, 60 percent of the CEOs admitted they did not have a corporate mission statement. For the rest who did, their mission statements were mostly drawn from templates and full of meaningless jargon.[3]

The official web site of Scott Adams' *Dilbert* once had an Automatic Mission Statement Generator that enabled users to craft mission statements by combining random bits of business jargon. Using the generator, you could develop thousands of mission statements that sounded ridiculous. This is one example: "*It is our job to continually foster world-class infrastructures as well as to quickly create principle-centered sources to meet our consumers' needs.*"[4] The generator is no longer available online but you would not want to use it anyway.

In this book, we will not offer you new templates or a new jargon generator. Our goal is to show you the key characteristics that make a good brand mission (see Figure 3.1). In Marketing 3.0, creating a good mission means introducing a new business perspective that can transform the lives of

Figure 3.1 Three Characteristics of a Good Mission

consumers. We call it "Business as Unusual," borrowing the well-known phrase from the late Anita Roddick, founder of The Body Shop. We also believe there is always a good story behind a good mission. Therefore, spreading the mission to consumers involves a story that moves people. An unusual idea embedded in a mission would have to reach mainstream market adoption to make a significant impact. In other words, realizing the mission requires consumer participation. Thus, consumer empowerment is crucial.

Business as Unusual

To find an original and innovative business idea is the dream of every start-up company. *Harvard Business Review* creates an annual list called the "Breakthrough Ideas" to report innovative ideas circulating around the world. But, what we really need is to find the ideas before they are known to be breakthrough by others. That requires a capability known as *strategic foresight*. This capability is rare and has always been found in the visionary and charismatic leaders who introduced great business ideas over the past decades (see Table 3.1 for a nonexhaustive list of visionary leaders and how they changed the conventional way of doing business). Their personal mission and their brand mission are inseparable and often the same. Visionary leaders are not necessarily innovators and pioneers. In fact, leaders such as Herb Kelleher, Anita Roddick, and even Bill Gates got their inspiration from other companies. But they were the ones who made the idea bigger and more meaningful to human lives.

Table 3.1 Examples of Business as Unusual Practices and Brand Missions of Visionary Leaders

Leader	Brand	Business as Unusual	Original Brand Mission
Ingvar Kamprad	IKEA	Invented the concept of foldable furniture and self-service experiential stores (in the 1960s) that made it possible for the furniture retailer to significantly save costs	Make stylish furniture affordable
Richard Branson	Virgin	Reinvented business with risky and diverse ventures under single brand name since 1970; applied unconventional business practices company-wide; most recently attempted to create commercial spacecraft with Virgin Galactic (2004)	Bring excitement to boring industries
Walt Disney	The Walt Disney Co.	Created successful animated characters and brought them into mainstream business with licensing and theme park experience	Create magical world for families
Herb Kelleher	Southwest Airlines	Although he got his ideas about the low-cost airline model and corporate culture from Pacific Southwest Airlines (established in 1949), Kelleher has brought low-cost airlines into the mainstream since 1971 and inspired worldwide adoption of the business model	Make flying possible for many people
Anita Roddick	The Body Shop	Although she copied the brand name and the idea of recycled packaging from a U.S. company in 1976 and had only accidentally practiced social activism 10 years later, Roddick introduced the idea of creating stories behind cosmetic products	Embed social activism in business

(continued)

Table 3.1 (*Continued*)

Leader	Brand	Business as Unusual	Original Brand Mission
Bill Gates	Microsoft	Although not an early pioneer, Gates has introduced operating systems into the mainstream since 1975 and arguably made software an essential part of computing by taking advantage of the network effect	Realize ubiquitous computing
Steve Jobs	Apple	Transformed the computing, music, and phone industries by introducing the Mac (1984), iPod (2001), and iPhone (2007) with cool counterculture approach; also reinvented animation pictures with Pixar (2006)	Transform how people enjoy technology
Jeff Bezos	Amazon.com	Reinvented retailing of books (and other products) with Amazon.com (1994) and reinvented the book itself with the Kindle (2007)	Provide the biggest selection of knowledge delivered conveniently
Pierre Omidyar	eBay	Connected sellers and buyers with eBay (1995), facilitated transaction and governance with user ratings and inclusion of PayPal as subsidiary (2002)	Create user-governed market space
Larry Page and Sergey Brin	Google	Since 1998, Google has been reinventing the search engine (the word "Google" is in the dictionary defined as a word for searching on the Internet); redefined online advertising by providing search engine-based advertising platform	Make the world's information organized and accessible

Table 3.1 (Continued)

Leader	Brand	Business as Unusual	Original Brand Mission
Jimmy Wales and Larry Sanger	Wikipedia	Since 2001, Wikipedia has been redefining the encyclopedia and popularizing the collaborative wiki approach developed by Ward Cunningham (1994)	Create a publicly editable encyclopedia
Mark Zuckerberg	Facebook	Although he did not invent social networking (Friendster was introduced first by Jonathan Abrams in 2002 and MySpace by Chris DeWolfe and Tom Anderson in 2003; Facebook was introduced later in 2004), Zuckerberg expanded the idea by introducing Facebook Platform (2007) and Connect (2008) and expanded social networking to a wider presence	Provide social network as business platform
Reid Hoffman	LinkedIn	LinkedIn introduced online professional networking and new ways of organizing professional contact information; some say it will soon replace the traditional resume for job search	Connect professionals around the world
Jack Dorsey	Twitter	Established in 2006, Twitter pioneered the idea of mini-blogs on the Internet and how people can broadcast their ideas to their network	Provide the tools to track friends and other interests

Those leaders who can make a huge impact from a small idea are the ones who really make a difference. Day and Schoemaker, who did extensive research on 119 global companies, argued that in an interlinked economy, the "butterfly effect" exists.[5] A small change in one part of the world can make big changes in other parts of the world. A business leader who captures this small change might gain significant advantage. To do this, leaders should not be operational leaders who focus on internal organization. They should be open for discovery and have outside-in mind-sets. Day and Schoemaker called these leaders "vigilant leaders"—the ones who have high levels of awareness, alertness, and willingness to undertake risky action based on small pieces of information. Michael Maccoby called them "narcissistic leaders": people who have narcissistic personalities that allow them to make bold decisions according to nonconsensus belief.[6]

We also put on our list that the brand missions are authentic and reflect what Peter Drucker argued: Businesses should start from a good mission.[7] Financial results come second. Amazon.com earned its first profit in 2001, after seven years of online existence.[8] Twitter has not even finalized its business model and is still not sure how to monetize its service.[9] Mark Zuckerberg insisted in 2007 that his focus was to build communities and not to exit and find a buyer for Facebook—like many other online start-ups did.[10] Although the financial goal is not their prime interest, they are all admirable brands with authentic missions and investment funds are lined up to support them.

Next, a good mission is always about change, transformation, and making a difference. Marketing 3.0 is about changing the way consumers do things in their lives. When a brand brings transformation, consumers will unconsciously accept the brand as part of their daily lives. This is what human spirit marketing is all about. In their book *The Experience Economy*, Pine and Gilmore argued that once the experience economy matures, it is time for the transformation economy to emerge.[11] We believe that the transformation economy—where a company's offering is a consumer's life-transforming experience—is already on its way.

Brand missions do not have to be complicated and sophisticated. In fact, they should be simple to allow for flexible business scoping. Look how visionary leaders pursue different strategies to fulfill their mission. Steve Jobs did it with the Mac, the iPod, and the iPhone, each influencing a different industry. Jeff Bezos launched the Kindle after successfully building Amazon.com. Companies need to continually rethink how to pursue their mission. To do that, they cannot rely on their founders forever. They need leaders at all levels. Some people argue that visionaries tend to be entrepreneurs. However, that should not discourage companies from encouraging intrapreneurs with visionary capabilities. General Electric has always been a benchmark for creating leaders within its organization, according to Noel Tichy.[12] The company launched the four-day Leadership, Innovation, and Growth (LIG) program in 2006 for top executives—specially designed to help GE develop leaders for its business expansion plans. According to GE CEO Jeff Immelt, the program is essential to embed growth in GE's corporate DNA, that is, its corporate mission.[13]

Story that Moves People

Robert McKee, a famous screenwriter, believes that there are two distinct ways to convince people.[14] The first one is to base your ideas on a set of facts and numbers and engage people in intellectual arguments. An alternative, which he thinks is much more effective, is to write compelling stories around the ideas and engage with people's emotions instead. When it comes to introducing a new product, Apple's Steve Jobs always chooses the second route. In fact, we can consider him as one of the master storytellers in business history. He always begins with a story. After the story is delivered, Jobs will then speak about the features and the set of facts regarding the product.

In the fall of 1983, the young Jobs aired the infamous "1984" commercial that would introduce the Macintosh to select audiences. He told a compelling story as to why 1984 was a year of transformation for the computing industry. He described the Macintosh as Apple's counter to IBM's attempt to dominate the computing industry. He argued that Apple was the only hope for dealers and consumers to avoid such dominance and enjoy the freedom of choice. In 2001, he engaged in another bit of brilliant storytelling. He introduced the iPod. The reason for being of the iPod was to let people carry the music libraries of their entire lives in their pockets. In 2007, he introduced the iPhone with the promise of transformation. The iPhone was portrayed as a revolutionary, smart, and easy-to-use device that combines music, phone, and the Internet. With his compelling stories, Steve Jobs has delivered the mission of transformation for the computing, music, and phone industries over the past 25 years.

But the stories that Jobs delivered were just the beginning. The complete stories of the Apple brand are the ones that have been continuously shaped in collaboration by multiple writers: the employees, channel partners, and most importantly the consumers. In the horizontal world, a big part of the story surrounding a brand is from collective wisdom. As stories are passed on from one writer to another, the stories are continuously rewritten. Companies can never be sure about the final stories circulating in the market. Hence, telling authentic stories in the beginning is always best.

A brand story, according to Holt, has at least three major components: character, plot, and metaphor.[15] A brand possesses great characters when it becomes the symbol of a movement that addresses the problems in the society and transforms people's lives. This is Holt's core theory about cultural branding. Once a brand becomes identified with a cultural movement, it becomes a cultural brand. For example, The Body Shop is the symbol of social activism while Disney is a symbol of family ideals. Wikipedia is the symbol of collaboration, while eBay is the symbol of user governance. In other words, a brand should promise business as unusual and deliver cultural satisfaction.

To make the characters relevant to people's lives, a good story needs a plot. In *Made to Stick*, Chip and Dan Heath offer three types of good story plots: challenge, connection, and creativity.[16] The story of David and Goliath is a classic example of a challenge plot. In this type of plot, a brand plays the role of a weaker protagonist that takes on the challenge against a stronger opponent or difficult obstacle. The brand, of course, wins at the end. The Body Shop makes a fine example of a challenge plot as it brings the stories of farmers in developing countries who fight for fair trade. Plots you find in the *Chicken Soup* book series are examples of connection plots. In this type of plot, the brand is bridging the gaps that exist in everyday lives: racial, age, gender, and so on. Social media brands like Facebook use the connection plot to spread their stories. The creativity plot, on the other hand, is typical of television's *MacGyver* series, in which MacGyver always finds a way to solve issues with his brilliance. Virgin is well known for using this type of story with Richard Branson playing the MacGyver character.

Most visionary leaders do not make up the stories. They simply spot the available ones floating around in everyday lives. Most stories are out there. That is what makes them sound and feel so relevant. But of course, you need to be sensitive to be able to capture the stories. To help you, Gerald and Lindsay Zaltman offer a process to reveal the deep metaphors.[17] Deep metaphors are encoded unconsciously in every human at a very young age. Using the Zaltman Metaphor Elicitation Technique (ZMET), we can pull out the metaphors to understand how to construct our stories and how consumers are likely to respond to the stories. Zaltman's seven metaphors, which represent 70 percent of all metaphors, are called the Seven Giants. They are *balance, transformation, journey, container, connection, resource,* and *control.*

In ZMET, consumers are asked to collect pictures and make a collage from those pictures. Through a systematic probing of the collages with the interviewees who collected them, we can interpret the deep metaphors embedded in the collage. For example, people who unconsciously use the balance metaphor, might make an expression about "overweight" when we probe their collage on diet or "equal employment" when we probe their collage on job search. These insights will be useful for companies whose mission it is to improve consumer diet or promote employment diversity. Understanding the sense of transformation that consumers have when switching, for instance, to the environmentally-friendly Prius during the Cash-for-Clunkers program, might be useful to create stories for Toyota. Consumers who use the journey metaphor, might, for instance, comment that "it is going to be an uphill task to survive in crisis." Understanding this helps companies build brand stories in times of recession.

The container metaphor can symbolize either protection or trap. People in impoverished rural areas see poverty as the trap that seals them off from outside opportunities, while senior employees see pension funds as the protection that guarantees their future survival. Metaphors can help companies understand the context in which consumers live. The connection metaphor is about relationship. Companies can reveal how consumers see other people in their networks. Companies can find the meaning of friendship or being a fan of one brand. Steve Jobs used the resource metaphor when he told the story that the iPhone would enable people to have the power of music, phone, and Internet in one device. The iPhone was positioned as a resource for the consumers. In an age of pandemics, consumers might express that they have no control over the spreading of diseases. What they can control is their own immunity. This is an example of the control metaphor.

Characters are central in a story. They symbolize how the brand is perceived by the human spirit. A plot structure shows how the character navigates among the network of humans who will rewrite their own version of the story. Metaphors are the unconscious process happening in the human spirit. Stories with compatible metaphors will gain relevancy and be perceived as truths by consumers. Stories that move people have all three of these core components: character, plot, and metaphor. Creating a good mission is a giant step for companies. Spreading it through storytelling is another.

Consumer Empowerment

Every year, *Time* compiles a list of the 100 most influential people in the world. The list never ranks the 100 most famous names, at least not officially. However, *Time* allows online readers to rank the list themselves. In the 2009 list, which includes the likes of Barack Obama and the late Ted Kennedy, the 21-year-old mysterious guy named "moot" is the champ. The creator of 4chan.org, an influential image-based online bulletin board, won the online poll way ahead of the others with over 16 million votes. According to *Time*, his web site gets 13 million page views a day and 5.6 million visitors a month.

In the horizontal world, people like to empower lesser known figures. They see the figure as a symbol of themselves: consumers with less power among the corporate giants. Giving consumers a sense of empowerment is therefore crucial in the pursuit of a brand mission. Show that the mission belongs to the consumers, and it is their responsibility to fulfill the mission. It is not only about getting buy-in but also about making an impact. Although the individual consumer is weak, their collective power will always be bigger than the power of any firm.

The value of consumers' collective power is rooted in the value of a network. The network may develop with one-to-one relationships, one-to-many relationships, or many-to-many relationships. When companies broadcast their brand stories through advertising, in the consumer network, the stories are spread one-to-one from one member to the other. Ethernet inventor Robert Metcalfe captured this in Metcalfe's Law when he argued that the power of a network of n members in a one-to-one setting is equal to n^2. However, Metcalfe's Law underestimates the power of networks when the relationship is one-to-many or many-to-many, that is, when consumers are having conversations with other consumers simultaneously. This is captured by Reed's Law, which is often used to explain the social media phenomenon.[18] According to Reed, the power of a network in a many-to-many environment of n members equals 2^n. Whenever n is greater than or equal to 5, the power of the many-to-many network is always bigger than that of the one-to-one network. This simple math is the central concept of consumer empowerment.

A great example of consumer empowerment is Google's Project 10^{100}. In celebration of its 10th birthday in September 2008, Google asked for ideas from consumers on how to help others in eight categories: community, opportunity, energy, environment, health, education, shelter, and everything else. Google will sort out 100 finalists and ask the public to vote for the best 20 ideas. The 5 best ideas selected by an advisory board will earn a total of $10 million dollars for implementation. The best idea is the one that can help the most people in the deepest way. Google takes advantage of the power of the network while practicing consumer empowerment. The response was immense and Google is still in the process of selecting the finalists.[19]

Even for low-consideration products such as consumer packaged goods, consumer empowerment in realizing a mission is a trend.[20] Colgate, a brand with a mission to make people smile, is running a consumer empowerment program called Smile. It encourages consumers to post photos of their smiles and connect with others participating in the program. Tide, a brand with a simple mission to clean clothes, has a program called Loads of Hope that lets people help others affected by disasters. Consumers can help Tide provide free mobile laundromats to disaster sites in multiple ways from making donations to volunteering.

Consumer empowerment is the platform for consumer conversation. Many-to-many conversation is what makes a consumer network so powerful. A brand story has no meaning when consumers are not talking about it. In Marketing 3.0, conversation is the new advertising. At Amazon.com it is common for readers to write reviews of books and recommend them to others. It is also common at eBay where people rate buyers and sellers and leave comments that determine their reputations. There is even a web site dedicated to reviews and recommendations called Yelp, and it is localized to your neighborhood. These are the early efforts to encourage consumer conversations. In a conversation, consumers review and give ratings to your brand and brand stories. Great reviews and ratings will influence the network to accept the stories.

People who are familiar with Amazon.com and eBay know that conversation can also be vicious as people can share their opinions bluntly. Consumers will find loopholes in any brand story. This type of consumer behavior poses a threat to companies that treat brand mission as a public relations tool or sales gimmick. But stories with strong integrity pose no reason for worry. They will earn their credibility in the network. Companies should not try to buy their way into conversation by sponsoring consumers to write bogus reviews. Consumers will consider this manipulation. According to Pine and Gilmore, companies that try to cheat on their consumers will be dubbed phoniness-generating machines.[21]

Conversation is not word-of-mouth or simply a recommendation. Positive word-of-mouth is recommendation given by delighted consumers. Frederick Reichheld offers a practical tool called the Net Promoter Score to measure loyalty based on the willingness of consumers to recommend a brand to their networks.[22] Because consumers who give recommendations will risk their own reputations, only strong brands will show high scores. It is a good measure of how active your brand is in the network of consumers. A high score is good news because most consumers rely on recommendation as a reason to buy. But it is not the complete story of conversation. Word of mouth is only one-to-one dialogue and it follows Metcalfe's Law. Conversation is many-to-many and it follows the more accurate Reed's Law.

Only brand stories that are talked about in the community will take advantage of the full power of the consumer network. A recent study by Wetpaint and the Altimeter Group showed that the most engaged brands in social networks increased their revenue by 18 percent.[23] Conversation is so powerful that brand stories remain strong even when the brand is in trouble. Consider the Saab community. In early 2010, Saab was in debt and its operations were about to be closed by General Motors. However, the stories of the brand such as, "how Saab saved my life," "the ritual of flashing lights to other Saab drivers," and "Snaabery hierarchy" remain topics of conversation.[24] Stories about a brand can live longer than the brand itself and create loyalty in consumers who see the brand as an icon.

SUMMARY: PROMISE OF TRANSFORMATION, COMPELLING STORIES, AND CONSUMER INVOLVEMENT

To market the company's or product's mission to consumers, companies need to offer a mission of transformation, build compelling stories around it, and involve consumers in accomplishing it. Defining a good mission starts with identifying small ideas that can make a big difference. Remember that mission comes first and financial return comes as a result. The best approach to spread the mission is through storytelling. Telling stories around the mission is about building character and plot based on metaphors. To convince consumers that your stories are authentic, engage them in conversation about your brand. Customer empowerment is the key to making a difference. These are the three principles of marketing the mission to consumers: *business as unusual*, a *story that moves people*, and *customer empowerment*.

NOTES

1. Anne B. Fisher, "Coke's Brand-Loyalty Lesson," *Fortune*, August 5, 1985.
2. Lisa Abend, "The Font War: IKEA Fans Fume over Verdana," *BusinessWeek*, August 28, 2009.
3. Jack Welch and Suzy Welch, "State Your Business: Too Many Mission Statements Are Loaded with Fatheaded Jargon. Play it Straight," *BusinessWeek*, January 14, 2008.
4. Paul B. Brown, "Stating Your Mission in No Uncertain Terms," *New York Times*, September 1, 2009.
5. George S. Day and Paul J.H. Schoemaker, "Are You a 'Vigilant Leader'?" *MIT Sloan Management Review*, Spring 2008, Vol. 49 No. 3.
6. Michael Maccoby, *Narcissistic Leaders: Who Succeeds and Who Fails* (Boston: Harvard Business School Press, 2007).
7. Peter F. Drucker, "What Business Can Learn from Nonprofits," *Classic Drucker* (Boston: Harvard Business School Press, 2006).
8. Saul Hansell, "A Surprise from Amazon: Its First Profit," *New York Times*, January 23, 2002.
9. Rafe Needleman, "Twitter Still Has No Business Model, and That's OK," *CNET News*, March 27, 2009.
10. Laura Locke, "The Future of Facebook," *Time*, July 7, 2007.
11. B. Joseph Pine II and James H. Gilmore, *The Experience Economy: Work Is Theater and Every Business a Stage* (Boston: Harvard Business Press, 1999).
12. Noel Tichy, *Leadership Engine: How Winning Companies Build Leaders at Every Level* (New York: HarperCollins, 2002).
13. Steven Prokesch, "How GE Teaches Teams to Lead Change," *Harvard Business Review*, January 2009.
14. "Storytelling that Moves People: A Conversation with Screenwriting Coach Robert McKee," *Harvard Business Review*, June 2003.
15. Douglas B. Holt, *How Brands Become Icons: The Principles of Cultural Branding* (Boston: Harvard Business School Press, 2004).
16. Chip Heath and Dan Heath, *Made to Stick: Why Some Ideas Survive and Others Die* (New Yok: Random House, 2007).

17. Gerald Zaltman and Lindsay Zaltman, *Marketing Metaphoria: What Deep Metaphors Reveal about the Minds of Consumers* (Boston: Harvard Business School Press, 2008).

18. David P. Reed, "The Law of the Pack," *Harvard Business Review*, February 2001.

19. For an update, visit the official web site at www.project10tothe 100.com.

20. Brian Morrissey, "Cause Marketing Meets Social Media," *Adweek*, May 18, 2009.

21. B. Joseph Pine and James H. Gilmore, "Keep It Real: Learn to Understand, Manage, and Excel at Rendering Authenticity," *Marketing Management*, January/February 2008.

22. Frederick F. Reichheld, "The One Number You Need to Grow," *Harvard Business Review*, December 2003.

23. Dan Schawbel, "Build a Marketing Platform like a Celebrity," *BusinessWeek*, August 8, 2009.

24. Sam Knight, "Insight: My Secret Love," *Financial Times*, July 25, 2009.

CHAPTER FOUR

Marketing the Values to the Employees

VALUES UNDER FIRE

The image of businesspeople has been greatly damaged in recent years. Many consumers have lost trust in major corporations and in their executives. In a 2009 survey of the image of different professions, only 16 percent of respondents said they respect the integrity of business executives.[1] The survey further revealed that marketing-related professions such as car salesmen and advertising executives were the least admired by the public. The most admired professions are the ones that make a more personal difference in people's lives like teachers, doctors, and nurses.

The survey's negative result is not surprising in light of events in the recent decade. Since the early 2000s, a string of corporate scandals has struck the business world. These scandals made corporate values almost meaningless to consumers and employees. Among the most prominent ones were the scandals at WorldCom, Tyco, and Enron. The Enron scandal was an accounting fraud that led the company into bankruptcy. Enron included unrealized gains into its income statement that resulted in inflated earnings—a practice known as mark-to-market accounting.

In the best-selling book on the fall of Enron, *The Smartest Guys in the Room*, you can read about the values of the company in 2000, a year before it went bankrupt.[2] Two of their four values were *respect* and *integrity*. Unfortunately, Enron's leaders did not practice these values at all. It was apparent that the accounting misconduct had been practiced for a long time and that the leaders were aware of the risks. In fact, Enron was considered a "deeply dysfunctional workplace where financial deception became almost inevitable."[3]

A more recent case was insurance company AIG's bonus controversy in March 2009. Huge bonuses were paid to AIG's executives using taxpayer money that bailed the company out of bankruptcy following the financial crisis. What makes it particularly ugly for the company's image is the fact that two of AIG's six corporate values—according to its Code of Conduct—are *respect* and *integrity*.[4] Although the executives finally returned the bonuses after a massive public outcry, they were in no way practicing *respect* and *integrity*. To make matters worse, AIG's executives charged the company with breaking trust with its employees. Jake DeSantis, an executive vice president of AIG, sent a resignation letter to the then AIG's CEO, Edward Liddy, that was also published in the *New York Times*:

> ...we in the financial products unit have been betrayed by AIG....I can no longer effectively perform my duties in this dysfunctional environment....You have now asked the current employees of AIG-FP to repay these earnings. As you can imagine, there has been a tremendous amount of serious thought and heated discussion about how we should respond to this breach of trust. As most of us have done nothing wrong, guilt is not a motivation to surrender our earnings.[5]

Clearly a company will take a beating from both the consumers and its employees over a violation of corporate values.

Some employees are ignorant of their corporate values or see them designed only for public relations. Some employees who really live up to the values are disappointed because other employees ignore them. In these cases, companies are not practicing Marketing 3.0. In Marketing 3.0, companies must convince both their customers and their employees to take their values seriously.

Employees are the most intimate consumers of the company's practices. They need to be empowered with authentic values. Companies need to use the same storytelling approach with their employees that they use with their consumers.[6] The use of metaphors that resonate with the human spirit works for employees as well. However, storytelling to employees is harder because it is about staging authentic and consistent employment experience. One misaligned action will spoil the entire story. Consumers can identify an inauthentic brand mission easily. Imagine how much easier it is for employees to spot fake values internally.

Privately-held companies usually have better chances at building strong values. They usually grow at the right pace without pressure from investors. They can ingrain their values one employee at the time. Attracting business is done within the framework of the company's values. Public companies can also achieve this practice of values as exemplified by such companies as IBM, General Electric, and Procter & Gamble. We believe that practicing corporate values will create the ProfitAbility, ReturnAbility, and SustainAbility that will be discussed later in Chapter 6.

VALUES DEFINED

According to Lencioni, there are four different types of corporate values.[7] *Permission-to-play values* are the basic standards of conduct that employees should have when they join the company. *Aspirational values* are values that a company lacks but the management hopes to achieve. *Accidental values* are acquired as a result of common personality traits of employees. *Core values* are the real corporate culture that guides employees' actions.

A company needs to distinguish these four types of values. Permission-to-play values are so basic that other companies have the same standard. The values of professionalism and integrity are normally assumed and therefore not core values but permission-to-play values. Moreover, remember that aspirational values are values that employees do not have as yet and therefore, cannot form the fundamental corporate culture. Nor can accidental values be treated as core values; they can alienate prospective employees with different personalities. Understanding the four types of values can help companies to design their core values better and avoid inauthentic ones.

We will talk only about the core values that guide employees to live up to the brand mission. We call them *shared values*. Shared values are one half of the corporate culture. The other half is the *common behavior* of employees. Shaping a corporate culture means aligning shared values and common behavior. In other words, it is about demonstrating the values through everyday behavior within the corporation (see Table 4.1 for examples[8]). The combination of employee values and behavior should reflect the company's brand mission. It is important to have employees acting as values ambassadors to market the brand mission to consumers.

Not all shared values are necessarily relevant and powerful in Marketing 3.0. Good values are the ones aligned with the forces at work: collaborative technology, globalization-driven cultural transformation, and the rising importance of creativity. Chapter 1 described these forces. In the interlinked world powered by information technology, people are increasingly collaborating to achieve one goal. Globalization causes cultural transformation to take place quickly and frequently. Finally, people are moving up Maslow's pyramid and becoming more creative. Hence, good values are those that stimulate and nurture the collaborative, cultural, and creative sides of employees (see Figure 4.1).

A company with collaborative values encourages employees to work with one another and with networks outside the

Table 4.1 Select Examples of Shared Values

Company	Select Shared Values	Select Common Behavior	Relevance in Marketing 3.0		
			Collaborative	Cultural	Creative
3M	Collaborative curiosity	Employees can spend a portion of their time collaborating and finding funding for pet projects; failure is embraced as a process of innovation.	●	◯	●
Cisco	Human network collaboration	Offices are labs for products. Employees are allowed to telecommute. Decision making is spread among hundreds of executives.	●	●	◐
Enterprise Rent-A-Car	Entrepreneurship	All executives, including the chairman and CEO, start as management trainees; good performers are given the chance to run a branch.	◐	●	◐
IDEO	Multidisciplinary creativity	Always assign multidisciplinary individuals to work in teams. Employees are given freedom to design their own workspace.	●	◐	●
Mayo Clinic	Integrated caring	Multiple physicians, scientists, and allied health professionals collaborate to diagnose and treat each patient.	●	●	◐
S.C. Johnson	Family values	No meetings on Fridays; employees who are couples have overseas assignments together.	◐	●	◐
Wegmans	Passion for food	Employees are trained to be food ambassadors and can purchase discounted gift cards to buy food.	◐	●	◐
Whole Foods	Democracy	Decisions made based on employee votes; stores are autonomous profit centers.	●	◐	◐

Note: Darker bullet means more relevance.

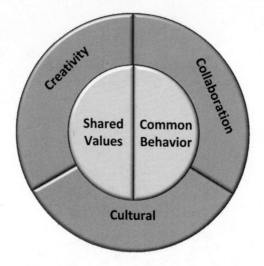

Figure 4.1 Shared Values and Common Behavior in Marketing 3.0 Context

company to make an impact. Cisco literally builds technical and human networks. The company uses its own offices as internal labs for products. Employees can telecommute using the company's network infrastructure. Decision making is spread among 500 executives worldwide. This enables Cisco to make critical decisions faster and empowers collaboration of its global executives. The company's values are mainly collaborative, but they also make cultural transformation by interlinking people globally.

The Mayo Clinic also fosters the values of collaboration. A number of physicians and other health experts come together to serve each patient. They collaborate to perform faster and more accurate diagnoses. They collaborate to treat the patient comprehensively. The culture of collaboration is what makes good physicians come to work for Mayo Clinic. By using the so-called Mayo Clinic Model of Care, the health care provider transforms the way doctors treat patients. Thus, it has cultural impact as well.[9]

Having cultural values means inspiring employees to make cultural changes in their own lives and the lives of others. Wegmans transforms the way people see food. Its employees are encouraged to appreciate food more deeply than ever before. The company also help consumers appreciate food. S.C. Johnson changes the way employees see family. They become better contributors to their families. The company develops products that are good for families. Whole Foods changes the way employees experience democracy. They feel more empowered as many decisions that affect employees are made through employee voting. Enterprise Rent-A-Car transforms college graduates into entrepreneurs by giving them the chance to run their own branches when they are ready. The company also transforms why people rent cars. At one time, people primarily rented cars in airports when they were traveling. Today, people can rent cars conveniently for many different reasons because there are so many car rental branches near their neighborhoods.

Finally, building creative values is about giving employees the chance to develop and share their innovative ideas. Companies such as 3M and IDEO rely on innovation as a major source of competitive advantage. In such companies, it is imperative to have creative employees. To nurture creativity, 3M allows employees to spend a portion of their time on pet projects. Employees can seek company funding for these projects and look for support from their colleagues. If successful, the outcome could be the company's next innovative product. Besides encouraging creativity, this policy also deepens collaboration among employees. There is the possibility of cultural transformation as well if the product can influence people's lives.

VALUES WILL DO YOU GOOD

Having great core values delivers several payoffs. A company with values has an advantage in competing for talent. It can attract better employees and retain them longer. The productivity of the employees is higher when they have a good set of values to guide their actions. Furthermore, they become better company representatives to serve consumers. The company is also more capable of managing differences within the organization, which is important especially for a large corporation.

Attracting and Retaining Talent

An influential 1997 survey by McKinsey & Company revealed that 58 percent of executives rated brand values and culture as the key motivation for employees.[10] In comparison, career advancement and growth only obtained a rating of 39 percent while differentiated compensation obtained 29 percent. This proves one thing: Good values attract good people. Prospective employees unconsciously compare their personal values with the values of corporations and look for a good fit.

This is especially true for recent graduates, many of whom are idealists. For instance, 50 percent of MBA graduates said in a poll that they were willing to take a pay cut to work in a socially-responsible company.[11] This is especially true in growing emerging markets. A recent study by Ready, Hill, and Conger focused on attracting and retaining talent in emerging markets.[12] They discovered that purpose and culture are among the most important factors for employees in Brazil, Russia, India, and China (BRIC). Emerging-market employees look for employers that provide the opportunity to change the world and bring cultural transformation to their home countries. They also are interested in employers that fulfill their brand promises internally, that is, companies with a good culture.

Once jobseekers are in the company, they will test the integrity of their employer. They will observe how companies demonstrate the values they proclaim. An employee survey by Tom Terez confirms that purpose is one of the meaningful experiences in the workplace. Companies that defend their values even when they hurt their business will earn admiration from their employees. One of the core values of the Bagel Works store is health and safety. To demonstrate its commitment to these values, the company buys smaller bags of flour to avoid back injuries to employees that carry them, although purchases in smaller packaging are more expensive.[13] It is imperative for companies to keep their integrity and practice what they preach. When employees witness the integrity of their employer, they are most likely to stay with full commitment. Well kept values improve employee loyalty.

A change of ownership of a company that might alter values has the potential to reduce the employee commitment. Consider the strong values held by Ben & Jerry's. After being purchased by Unilever in 2000, the values remained strong. However, as reported in the company's social and environmental assessment report in 2007, the commitment of employees had lessened, perhaps due to continued concern over the future of the company's values under Unilever.[14] This anxiety was also felt when The Body Shop was bought by L'Oreal. Employees recognized the increased growth potential. But the question is whether the values will be maintained. This is especially true for companies that had a strong tradition of practicing corporate values such as Ben & Jerry's and The Body Shop.[15]

Back-Office Productivity and Front-Office Quality

The happiness of employees has a significant impact on their productivity. Companies listed in *The Sunday Times'* "100 Best Companies to Work For" outperform the FTSE All-Share Index by between 10 percent and 15 percent.[16] Employees are more productive when they believe in what their company tries to achieve. They will commit their minds, hearts, and spirits. Starbucks' Howard Schultz called this "pouring your heart into it" when referring to employees' commitment.

Porter and Kramer argue that companies with a social purpose can gain advantage by shaping their competitive environment.[17] For instance, Marriott is educating its employees who may come from backgrounds of limited education. By adding education as part of its values, Marriott is able to hire better and more productive employees.

Values-driven employees not only work harder but also become a better face of the company. They deliver consumer value that is aligned with their company's stories. Their beliefs shape their common behavior in everyday work especially when interacting with consumers. Their behavior will be part of the brand stories that customers talk about. Companies should see their employees as values ambassadors. Consumers will judge the authenticity of companies by judging their employees.

When Wegmans declares that the company understands food better than others, consumers' in-store experience will determine the integrity of the claim. Wegmans employees are trained to be food ambassadors. The company helps its employees appreciate food. The employees know the details of all the food they sell. As a result, employees are empowered to educate consumers about food when they interact in stores. They deliver the integrity of the brand story.

The best salespeople are those who use their own product and understand it inside out. At Cisco, the network company, employees experience daily what it means to be well-connected to everyone in their company and its network. Everyday work is like product training for them. Thus, they can deliver convincing and realistic stories to their prospective clients about the benefit of human interconnection. Employees are empowered to tell the brand story because they are living the story. Nicholas Ind calls this "living the brand."[18]

Integrating and Empowering Differences

A study of large corporations by Rosabeth Moss Kanter revealed that strong shared values help companies accomplish seemingly opposing goals.[19] A big corporation has multiple offices with diverse employees. Shared values reduce the differences and integrate the employees in one corporate culture. Strong values that are internalized by every employee give the company the confidence to empower its employees, including the ones who are distant from the corporate headquarters. Those employees will commit all their actions to benefit the company. Companies with strong shared values usually succeed with decentralized or localized decision making. These values help companies not only to standardize but to localize as well.

Enterprise Rent-A-Car is a classic example of this. Unlike Avis and Hertz that compete mostly in airports, Enterprise has a strong presence in local neighborhood markets. The culture that it fosters ensures its success. All Enterprise employees embody the strong values of hard-working and friendly entrepreneurs. Enterprise uses a long-standing routine to create this culture: Recruit new college graduates, tell them to work hard by washing and shuttling cars, teach them how to build long-term relationships with customers, let them progress up the ranks, and give them a branch to run when they are ready.[20] Employees that pass through this routine will come out as hard-working entrepreneurs. The humility that employees pick up while washing and shuttling cars as well as building relationships transforms them into friendly people. These employees have the same values but each one of them has unique local knowledge. The values enable Enterprise not only to create customized local strategies but also to coordinate the strategies of different markets. The values are so difficult to imitate that Enterprise continues to maintain its lead in the local markets.

Values also integrate and empower diversity at the same time. Looking at the annual list of the Fortune 100 Best Companies to Work For, we see a group of companies that nurture diversity by hiring women and minorities. The companies' shared values unify the diverse employees under one culture. That diversity will be sustained without creating conflicts because of the shared values.

PRACTICE WHAT YOU PREACH

To instill values, most companies rely on formal training and informal coaching. Values training is necessary but it may have some weaknesses. The training can turn into preaching instead of practicing. Trainers and coaches might not act as role models in their everyday activities in the workplace. Employees might see this and realize the value talk is largely just words. Furthermore, employees tend to listen passively and have less opportunity to contribute. Their understanding is also limited because they have not experienced the values through practice.

Marketing 3.0 is about more than just training and coaching. It is about aligning values with behavior. According to Jim Collins, there are two parts to creating such alignment.[21] First, a company should examine current corporate policies that might weaken corporate values. This is challenging because most corporate policies are more institutionalized than corporate values themselves. Changing them requires action by the company's leaders and collaboration with all employees. Most of the time, employees have the same sense of the corporate practices that they misaligned. But unless you empower them, they will not say anything. Second, a company should create a mechanism that directly links actions with values. For instance, a company can create a mechanism that requires 30 percent of revenues to come from new products to strengthen the value of innovation. Marketing 3.0 is about transforming employees and empowering employees to transform others.

Change the Lives of Employees

S.C. Johnson's values as a fifth-generation family company are, of course, family values. The company is putting a lot of effort into promoting the values not only to consumers but also to employees. To work in a company with family values is to lead a balanced family-work lifestyle. That is what employees get from S.C. Johnson. A man and his wife, both working at S.C. Johnson, can expect to get an overseas assignment together.[22] At S.C. Johnson, there are no business meetings on Fridays so that employees can go home early for family weekends.[23] Working at S.C. Johnson can transform employees into family people. The company's values have a direct impact on employees' lives. Erickson and Gratton call it creating "signature experience within an organization." Creating a signature experience requires understanding the motivation of employees. Studies by Erickson, Dychtwald, and Morrison reveal six segments of employees:

1. The *low obligation and easy income* segment is a group of employees who look for quick wins.

2. The *flexible support* segment is a group that goes with the flow because they do not see a job as a priority yet.

3. The *risk and reward* segment includes employees who see jobs as opportunities to challenge and excite themselves.

4. The *individual expertise and team success* segment seeks jobs that offer teamwork and collaboration.

5. The *secure progress* segment looks for a promising career path.

6. The *expressive legacy* segment looks for opportunities to create a lasting impact on the company.[24]

This segmentation is somewhat similar to the employee segmentation framework that McKinsey & Company developed.[25] That study distinguished four types of employees. *Go with a winner* employees look for growth and achievement. *Big risk big reward* employees look for good compensation. *Lifestyle* employees seek flexibility. Finally, *save the world* employees seek opportunities to contribute to a great mission.

Understanding employee segmentation gives companies the inspiration to design the signature experience for their target segment. It also helps companies weed out unsuitable employees who will likely deviate from the values and ruin the experience of the suitable ones. In Marketing 3.0, signature experience should be collaborative, cultural, or creative.

Companies should target specific segments that their core values can best satisfy. An adventurous company with creative values might be suitable for the risk and reward (or big risk big reward) segment. Companies with cultural values that offer the opportunity to market their products to poor people would suit the expressive legacy (or save the world). The individual expertise and team success segment is the right target segment for companies with collaborative values that offer opportunities to work with other people around the world.

Empower Employees to Make Change

A Chinese proverb says, *"Tell me and I'll forget; show me and I may remember; involve me and I'll understand."* This is relevant to employee empowerment. Employees need to be involved and empowered. Their lives have been changed by the company's values. Now, it is their turn to change the lives of others. It is about creating a platform for employees to make a difference.

Employee empowerment can come in various forms. The most common one is volunteering. In Volunteering for Impact, Hills and Mahmud argue that volunteering achieves high impact when there is a strategic impact that leverages the company's resources.[26] In her book *SuperCorp*, Kanter discusses an example focusing on IBM.[27] When the tsunami and earthquake hit Asia in December 2004, employees of IBM pushed forward an innovation whose mission was to help the victims. While the company had no initial business interest when it launched the effort, the innovation later brought commercial payoff. A SuperCorp, according to Kanter, is a vanguard company that has bigger societal purposes embedded in how they make money. They make a strategic impact when working for a social purpose. High-impact volunteering is one way to be a SuperCorp.

Another form of empowerment is through innovation. IDEO is famous for developing some of the best product designs in the world. To achieve this, according to founder David Kelly, IDEO moved up the Maslow pyramid and introduced human-centered design in which IDEO brings performance and personality into products. IDEO assigns a project to a multidisciplinary team with a marketer, psychologist, physician, anthropologist, economist, and others to develop innovative products that solve their clients' problems. IDEO brings this approach one step further by making its proprietary methodology available to those outside the firm. The company creates an open-source toolkit to develop solutions for social problems in developing nations in cooperation with the Gates Foundation and many other nonprofit organizations.

Empowerment can also mean sharing power. In Marketing 3.0, the role of leaders is to inspire. They are not necessarily the sole decision makers. Companies such as Cisco and Whole Foods practice collaborative democracy where employees are given opportunities to shape the future of the company through decision making and voting. In these cases, companies are increasingly becoming communities. In communities, decisions are made together to advance the common interests of the members.

SUMMARY: SHARED VALUES AND COMMON BEHAVIOR

In Marketing 3.0, corporate culture is about integrity. It is about aligning the shared values and common behavior of employees. In the context of the forces at work, corporate culture should be collaborative, cultural, and creative. It should transform the lives of employees and empower employees to transform the lives of others. By building their integrity, companies can compete in the talent market, improve productivity and the consumer interface, and manage differences. Marketing its values to employees is as important as marketing the mission to consumers.

NOTES

1. Gina McColl, "Business Lacks Respect," *BRW*, Vol. 31, Issue 25, June 25, 2009.

2. Bethany McLean and Peter Elkind, *The Smartest Guys in the Room: The Amazing Rise and Scandalous Fall of Enron* (New York: Portfolio, 2003).

3. Sarah F. Gold, Emily Chenoweth, and Jeff Zaleski, "The Smartest Guys in the Room: The Amazing Rise and Scandalous Fall of Enron," *Publishers Weekly*, Vol. 250, Issue 41, October 13, 2003.

4. Alaina Love, "Flawed Leadership Values: The AIG Lesson," *BusinessWeek*, April 3, 2009.

5. Jake DeSantis, "Dear AIG, I Quit!" *New York Times*, March 25, 2009.

6. Neeli Bendapudi and Venkat Bendapudi, "How to Use Language that Employees Get," *Harvard Business Review*, September 2009.

7. Patrick M. Lencioni, "Make Your Values Mean Something," *Harvard Business Review*, July 2002.

8. Information is gathered from multiple sources, mainly the companies' web sites as well as *Fortune* and *Fast Company* magazines.

9. Leonard L. Berry and Kent D. Seltman, *Management Lessons from Mayo Clinic: Inside One of the World's Most Admired Service Organizations* (New York: McGraw-Hill, 2008).

10. Elizabeth G. Chambers, Mark Foulon, Helen Handfield-Jones, Steve M. Hankin, and Edward G. Michaels III, "The War for Talent," *The McKinsey Quarterly*, Number 3, 1998.

11. David Dorsey, "The New Spirit of Work," *Fast Company*, July 1998.

12. Douglas A. Ready, Linda A. Hill, and Jay A. Conger, "Winning the Race for Talent in Emerging Markets," *Harvard Business Review*, November 2008.

13. Brian R. Stanfield, "Walking the Talk: The Questions for All Corporate Ethics and Values Is: How Do They Play Out in Real Life?" *Edges Magazine*, 2002.

14. Social and Environmental Assessment 2007, accessed online at www.benjerry.com/company/sear/2007/index.cfm, Ben & Jerry's, 2008.

15. "The Body Beautiful—Ethical Business," *The Economist*, March 26, 2006.
16. William B. Werther, Jr. and David Chandler, *Strategic Corporate Social Responsibility: Stakeholders in a Global Environment* (Thousand Oaks, CA: Sage Publications, 2006).
17. Michael E. Porter and Mark R. Kramer, "Strategy & Society: The Link between Competitive Advantage and Corporate Social Responsibility," *Harvard Business Review*, December 2006.
18. Nicholas Ind, *Living the Brand: How to Transform Every Member of Your Organization into a Brand Champion* (London: Kogan Page, 2007).
19. Rosabeth Moss Kanter, "Transforming Giants," *Harvard Business Review*, January 2008.
20. Brian O'Reilly, "The Rent-a-Car Jocks Who Made Enterprise #1," *Fortune*, October 26, 1996.
21. Jim Collins, "Align Action and Values," *Leadership Excellence*, January 2009.
22. Chris Murphy, "S.C. Johnson Does More than Talk," *Information Week*, 19 September 2005.
23. Robert Levering, "The March of Flextime Transatlantic Trends," *Financial Times*, April 28, 2005.
24. Tamara J. Erickson and Lynda Gratton, "What It Means to Work Here," *Harvard Business Review*, March 2007.
25. Charles Fishman, "The War for Talent," *Fast Company*, December 18, 2007.
26. Greg Hills and Adeeb Mahmud, "Volunteering for Impact: Best Practices in International Corporate Volunteering," FSG Social Impact Advisor, September 2007.
27. Rosabeth Moss Kanter, *SuperCorp: How Vanguard Companies Create Innovation, Profits, Growth, and Social Good* (New York: Random House, 2009).

CHAPTER FIVE

Marketing the Values to the Channel Partners

GROWTH MIGRATION AND COLLABORATION IMPERATIVE

Dell revolutionized the computer industry by introducing the direct model of distribution. Consumers could order customized computers and have them delivered directly. Dell would maintain a direct relationship with consumers, bypass resellers, and keep all the margin. Due to Dell's famous cut-out-the-middleman principle, the company was considered an enemy by the middleman—the resellers. Competitors were at first unconvinced by this business model but later tried to copy it without any luck. The solo run worked so well without meaningful rivalry that, by 1999, Dell was the largest seller on the Internet ahead of Amazon.com, eBay, and Yahoo! combined.[1]

Everything has changed since 2005. To Dell's surprise, the world changed. Growth started to stall. Dell's stock tumbled. First, the U.S. market was starting to mature. Experts were pushing Dell to embrace the middleman to solve this problem. Sunil Chopra was one of them when he argued that in mature markets, consumers increasingly saw computers as commodities and were less concerned about customization.[2]

Chopra recommended that Dell either try the direct-indirect hybrid model or do the customization model through resellers. In either model, Dell should start collaborating with the middleman.

The second reason for Dell's setback was that Dell relied on extracting value from its direct relationship with consumers. When the market matured, however, its customers found other attractive computers. Dell could have focused on other growth markets such as China and India. Unfortunately, in these markets, most consumers do not buy computers online.[3] They prefer high-touch human interface more than high-tech Internet interface. The direct business model failed to accommodate consumer needs in growth markets. Again, it was imperative for Dell to pursue a completely opposite business model: indirect distribution.

Although the company did not admit it, in 2002, Dell had actually complemented the direct model with indirect distribution through solution providers that served corporate consumers.[4] But 2005 was the tipping point. Dell quietly began building relationships with resellers who initially distrusted the company. The move started to pay off. By mid-2007, Dell's sales through channels had risen to account for 15 percent of its overall revenue, although no official partnership was announced.[5] In December 2007, Dell finally launched the PartnerDirect program and revealed that it had built partnerships with 11,500 partners and was adding 250 to 300 a week.[6]

It was apparent that in the last few years Dell had managed to transform its key capability of building direct relationships with consumers into the capability of building direct relationships with channel partners. Dell approached resellers one by one, listened to their feedback, and invited them to have conversations in the Partner Advisory Council meetings. Michael Dell himself personally showed up to the meetings to convince skeptical channel partners. Once a nemesis of the channel, Dell is now embracing its new partners with the kind of attention that it gives to consumers.

The story of Dell reflects the opposing forces that exist in the business world. Technology enabled Dell to capture the value of direct distribution. But technology also enabled the forces of globalization to work. The most value is no longer in the developed market but in the developing markets where technology adoption has not reached its mainstream potential. The developing market requires different business approaches where traditional distribution might not work. Social, economic, and environmental problems are abundant in these markets and need to be addressed before a company tries to build a new distribution network. Entering unknown territories, companies are forced to collaborate with new partners.

The developed market, too, is transforming into a completely different kind of market. The maturing market is just a small signal of the big changes that are taking place. As society becomes more sophisticated, consumers will try to satisfy higher human needs and basic needs become secondary. Consumers will give more consideration to social, economic, and environmental impacts. James Speth viewed this phenomenon as the era of post-growth society.[7] It may happen that customization will no longer be that important to consumers. These post-growth changes are essential for Dell and other companies to understand, as they have serious implications for their marketing channel practices.

CHANNEL PARTNERS IN MARKETING 3.0

We view channel partners as complex entities. They are hybrids of companies, consumers, and employees. They are also companies with their own missions, visions, values, and business models. They are consumers with needs and wants that need to be served. Moreover, they also sell to end-users and form the consumer interface just like employees do. Their role is essential in Marketing 3.0 as they become collaborators, cultural change agents, and creative partners for companies at the same time.

Channel as Collaborator: Selecting the Fit

Companies that have a difficult time managing their channel partners perhaps did not choose their partners appropriately. In Marketing 3.0, channel partner selection requires the process of mirroring the Purpose-Identity-Values. Mirroring means that companies should select potential partners that have identical Purpose-Identity-Values (see Figure 5.1).

Purpose relates to the overall key objective of a potential channel partner and is relatively easy to observe and research. Identity relates more to the character of a potential partner and therefore requires a deeper investigation to understand. Values are even more difficult to observe because

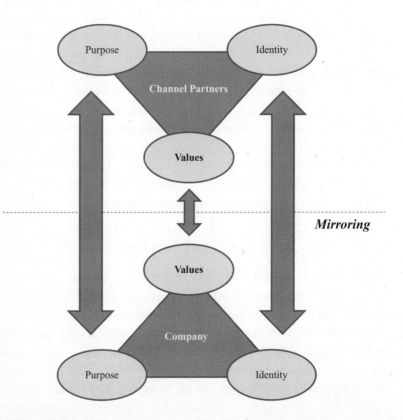

Figure 5.1 Selecting Compatible Channel Partners

they involve the shared beliefs within the channel partner organization.

In its early years, The Body Shop grew mainly because of its store franchises. The company was built on the naïve character of the late Anita Roddick. The founder's honesty and simplicity are reflected in all facets of the company's business as seen in its descriptive product naming, use of natural ingredients, and fair trade with suppliers. When Roddick was selling her products in her own store, there was no problem because she could apply her non-mainstream approach independently. But when the imperative to grow emerged, she had to move to a multi-channel approach and find franchisees as her channel partners.

Her approach to selecting channel partners was very personal. She did the final interviews herself, and during each interview, tried to understand the character of the potential channel partner. What she was looking for were people who were more interested in making a difference than making a profit. She discovered that women were more likely than men to share her same social and environmental values. That was why in the early years, 90 percent of The Body Shop franchisees were women. The franchising approach was unquestionably successful. The Body Shop grew at about 50 percent annually during the first decade of its existence.[8]

Compare this story to the partnerships Ben & Jerry's established in Russia before the company's acquisition by Unilever. Like The Body Shop, Ben & Jerry's was also founded as a socially-responsible company. It also started by selling a simple homemade product: ice cream. Because of its long-term vision of making the world a better place, the early management of Ben & Jerry's had no interest in aggressive growth. The preference was always to have someone from inside the company who really understood the company's values lead moderate business expansion.

Although ice cream was very popular in Russia, it was not because of business considerations that Ben & Jerry's entered the country. Not aiming for profit, Ben & Jerry's just wanted to strengthen the relationship between the United States and Russia in the aftermath of the Cold War the two countries had waged for many years. When Ben & Jerry's decided to establish a foothold on Russian soil in the 1990s, they assigned someone from the United States who could be trusted: Dave Morse. But Morse could not work alone. He needed channel partners.

In Russia, Dave Morse found it difficult to find suitable partners to grow the brand. Potential partners were plenty but none of them really understood the socially-responsible values of Ben & Jerry's. The potential partners were ambitious, profit-oriented companies that pursued aggressive growth. The partners had a strong belief that the Ben & Jerry's brand would be a valuable asset to them but lacked understanding of its fundamentals. In the end, Ben & Jerry's decided to partner with Intercentre Cooperative to bring the brand to Russia.

Right from the start, it was obvious that the partners were not perfect. Ben & Jerry's and its partners were heading in two different directions. Their business values were not aligned. Aiming for instant success, the partners wanted to build the business in Moscow straight away. But the management of Ben & Jerry's wanted to start humbly in small-town Petrozavodsk to mirror their U.S. start-up in small-town Vermont. Ben & Jerry's and the Russian partners also had conflicting opinions about bribery, which was common in Russia at that time. The quality of the partners' sourcing for environmentally-friendly ingredients was also below the high expectation of Ben & Jerry's management.[9]

Rackham, Friedman, and Ruff emphasized the importance of shared values.[10] They pointed out three key assessments to determine the potential success of partnership. First, both entities in a partnership should ask themselves whether both of them desire a win-win outcome. Good partnership creates a horizontal relationship, not a vertical one. Each entity should derive an equitable benefit from the collaboration. Second, they should investigate whether both business entities uphold a high quality standard. Companies with the same approach to quality will have a better chance in building partnership. Finally, each business entity should identify its potential partner's unique values and determine the compatibility with its own unique values.

Research by Cui, Raju, and Zhang also confirms the importance of shared values.[11] When the value of fairness exists in the partnership between the company and its channel partners, it is easier to coordinate price stability across the channel structure and therefore improve overall channel economics. When a company sets a fair trade price, the channel partners will respond accordingly by establishing a fair end-user price in the market. This fair partnership mechanism is enabled by increased transparency of cost information between the company and its channel partners.

The first step for a company marketing its values to its channel partners is to understand the partners' own values. In Marketing 3.0, collaboration between two business entities is like a marriage between two human beings. Mirroring the purpose, values, and identities—beyond understanding each other's business model, applying win-win negotiation, and writing sound legal contracts—is essential. That is why the personal approach, exemplified by Anita Roddick, is always the best.

Channel Partners as Cultural Change Agent: Distributing the Story

The growth imperative requires a company to have channel partners manage their consumer interface. Therefore, the company becomes highly dependent on the distributors to market its values, especially when the company does not communicate directly to the consumers through promotional media. Look at the Maria Yee case, for example. Almost half of the furniture sold in the United States in 2007 was channeled through furniture retailers.[12] Maria Yee, Inc., like other furniture manufacturers, markets products to the upper-middle market through three key retailers: Crate & Barrel, Room

& Board, and Magnolia Home Theater. The company itself focuses on selling eco-friendly products. The values of being green are clearly demonstrated in the company's business model, especially in the use of sustainable materials and in the partnership with eco-friendly suppliers.

Unfortunately, Maria Yee does not have a direct interface with consumers and therefore relies on its channel partners to send its "green" messages. To keep the green values alive and lead the eco-friendly movement in the industry, Maria Yee, the founder herself, maintains personal relationships with the retailers. The role of retailers is not only to communicate the brand positioning of Maria Yee to consumers but also to promote the overall benefits of using eco-friendly furniture. Normally, green products are perceived by consumers to be more expensive. Maria Yee relies on its channel partners to convince consumers otherwise. Channel partners themselves have to be convinced that Maria Yee's products remain competitive in pricing.

In contrast, a large consumer packaged goods (CPG) company often creates direct touch points with the consumers although it is also fully dependent on channel partners for distribution. Stonyfield Farm, a company that produces organic yogurt products, sells all its products through distributors to natural food stores and supermarkets. Nevertheless, the wellness-oriented company tries to create direct contact with consumers to market the company's social and environmental mission. It formed myStonyfield community to create favorable word-of-mouth. It uses YouTube to send its message to consumers.

Spreading brand stories through channel partners requires a consistent personal approach. When it does not work, companies should begin convincing the channel partners by means of signaling. By spreading the stories directly to the consumers, companies can generate interest. When a lot of consumers respond and look for the brand in channel outlets, this sends a strong signal to the channel partners that the values have a strong impact on the brand and that carrying the brand is good for them.

In some cases, the consumers themselves are channel partners. This is especially true when distributing to low-income consumers in developing markets. In developing countries, the biggest issue of marketing to the poor is access. Two elements of the marketing mix that are most affected by the lack of access are place (distribution) and promotion (communication). Many products and information are not readily accessible to the poor, especially in rural areas. Channeling products to these consumers will increase market penetration and, at the same time, improve their lives. Vachani and Smith call this socially-responsible distribution.[13]

India is a place where socially responsible distribution is best modeled. The country has been struggling to eradicate poverty. Looking at the statistics, the result is promising. The percentage of people living in poverty decreased from 60 percent in 1981 to 42 percent in 2005.[14] One of the key success factors lies in the effort to increase access to the poor. This can be seen from the fact that rural consumers accounted for around 80 percent of total consumer spending in India.[15] In the process of fighting poverty, companies that operate in India are developing innovative methods of distribution utilizing networks of humans.

Companies such as ITC and Hindustan Lever play a significant role in partnering with the poor to distribute their products in the rural areas. ITC is famous for developing the e-Choupal, which enables farmers to access information on weather and crop prices and sell their produce directly to consumers without middlemen. Leveraging its network of farmer partners, ITC also developed the Choupal Saagars, a network of mini-malls that sell products ranging from consumer goods to health and financial services. Hindustan Lever, on the other hand, empowers a community of rural women to sell consumer goods. Being distribution partners of Hindustan Lever enables the women to earn additional incomes. In different ways, the two companies are selling their socially-responsible values to their channel partners who happen to be their consumers as well.

What ITC and Hindustan Lever are doing is understandable considering that 87 percent of consumers in India purchase a product on the basis of recommendation from family and friends.[16] That is the key reason why peer-to-peer selling is the most commonly applied go-to-market strategy in India, especially when targeting the rural market.

In new growth markets, distribution relies on networks of many channel partners. The innovative distribution model is rooted in the emerging phenomenon of communitization of consumers. The consumers' role is not only limited to promoting brands but is extended to selling them. In extreme cases such as in India, channel partners are individual consumers. In less extreme cases, channel partners are small enterprises that have better local knowledge and personal access with communities of consumers. These channel partners are the best media to send the brand stories to consumers because they have more credibility. Consumers listen to them. Companies, such as Dell, that look for growth markets should embrace this emerging trend.

Channel as Creative Ally: Managing the Relationship

In Marketing 3.0, the power belongs to the consumers. Unfortunately, not all companies have direct access to the consumers. Generally, there are intermediaries between them and their consumers. These channel partners not only distribute the products to the market but also provide a consumer touch point. In some cases, channel partners are perceived to be more important than the manufacturers. In the IT industry, for example, consumers often have better relationships with value-added resellers than with the manufacturers. The value-added resellers are perceived to be capable of delivering solutions, while manufacturers only sell commodity components.

This growing importance of channel partners demands that companies take more factors into consideration when managing their partners. First, companies should understand their products' margin contribution, inventory turnaround rate, and general strategic importance to the channel partners. Second, companies should demonstrate genuine concern and active management of the "selling out" process at the retail level through co-op marketing, in-store promotion, and ensuring a brand's presence in retail outlets. Finally, a company should also care about and understand its channel partners' general impressions and satisfaction.

This concept of company-channel integration is particularly important in cases where channels are becoming an increasingly important link in the value chain, to the point that many channels and companies today are engaged in competition for consumer loyalty and ownership. Without the presence of such integration in the value chain, companies and channels will likely engage in a zero-sum game of rivalry for margins and consumer influence instead of working together in mutual cooperation to find and employ synergistic opportunities to go up against other competitors.

Company-channel integration usually starts from basic cooperation between a company and its channel partners, especially in retail promotion. As the relationship strengthens, they start to integrate with one another and also with other members of their industry's value chain. The integration process involves regular information sharing and joint strategic planning. When the partnership moves forward to the next stage, their values unite and we can see no differences between the company and the channel partners.

When it comes to creative channel partnership, we observe four stages of excellence. A company is at the first stage when it is dependent on one channel, whether a direct sales force or a sole channel partner, for its entire sales effort. This is the Single Channel stage. Many companies start out in a limited regional setting where all sales can be covered by their own sales force or a single channel partner.

As the company grows, it adds more distributors and other channels to increase its coverage area to improve sales revenue and product availability without limiting where or to whom each distributor or other channel may sell. This strategy normally results in sales conflict among the distributors and other channels. This second stage is the Multi-Channel stage, in which the company sells to multiple distributors and direct channels but does not delineate product, segment, or geographical boundaries.

A more advanced distribution systems takes into consideration channel conflict problems and divides the company's market by territories, consumer segments, or product segments. Each distributor or channel is then given a separate piece of the market to develop. This third level is the Territory-Based Channel stage, in which the company sets clear boundaries and rules for distributors and direct channels to operate to avoid channel conflict.

In the most advanced distribution systems, there exists a division of tasks among a company's various channels. With this division of tasks, several different types of channels can coexist within a segment or regional market. Instead of competing with each other, the channels will collaborate. This fourth level is the Integrated Multi-Channel stage, in which a company divides tasks between different channels. Multiple channels may coexist within a regional market or market segment by working together and not competing for business. For example, a computer manufacturer may allocate tasks to multiple channels: a web site to generate demand, its own stores to stage consumer experience, resellers to distribute and provide technical support, and a sales force to sell to corporate consumers and provide referrals to the nearest resellers. Companies should try to achieve this most advanced degree of integration. In the Integrated Multi-Channel stage, the company and its channel partners creatively find new ways to serve the consumers without conflict.

SUMMARY: VALUES-DRIVEN CHANNEL PARTNERSHIP

In Marketing 3.0, channel management begins with finding the right channel partners with similar purpose, identity, and ultimately values. Partners with compatible values will be able to deliver the stories convincingly to consumers. To bring the partnership one step further, companies should integrate with the partners to bring integrity to the stories.

NOTES

1. Andrew Park, "Michael Dell: Thinking Out of the Box," *Business-Week*, November 24, 2004.
2. Sunil Chopra, "Choose the Channel that Matches Your Product," *Supply Chain Strategy*, 2006.
3. Olga Kharif, "Dell: Time for a New Model," *BusinessWeek*, April 6, 2005.
4. Mitch Wagner, "IT Vendors Embrace Channel Partners," *BtoB*, September 9, 2002.
5. Paul Kunert, "Dell in Channel Embrace," *MicroScope*, May 7, 2007.
6. Scott Campbell, "Dell and the Channel: One Year Later," *Computer Reseller News*, August 11, 2008.
7. James Gustave Speth, "Doing Business in a Post-Growth Society," *Harvard Business Review*, September 2009.
8. The complete story of The Body Shop can be found in Christopher Bartlett, Kenton Elderkin, and Krista McQuade, "The Body Shop International," Harvard Business School Case, 1995.
9. The complete story of Ben & Jerry's in Russia can be found in Iris Berdrow and Henry W. Lane, "Iceverks: Ben & Jerry's in Russia," Richard Ivey School of Business Case, 1993.
10. Neil Rackham, Lawrence Friedman, and Richard Ruff, *Getting Partnering Right: How Market Leaders Are Creating Long-Term Competitive Advantage* (New York: McGraw-Hill, 1996).
11. Tony Haitao Cui, Jagmohan S. Raju, and Z. John Zhang, "Fairness and Channel Coordination," *Management Science*, Vol. 53, No. 8, August 2007.
12. Maria Shao and Glenn Carrol, "Maria Yee Inc.: Making 'Green' Furniture in China," Stanford Graduate School of Business Case, 2009.
13. Sushil Vachani and N. Craig Smith, "Socially Responsible Distribution: Strategies for Reaching the Bottom of the Pyramid," *California Management Review*, 2008.

14. "New data show 1.4 billion live on less than $1.25 a day, but progress against poverty remains strong," http://go.worldbank.org/DQKD6WV4T0 World Bank, 2008.

15. Sushil Vachani and N. Craig Smith, "Socially Responsible Distribution: Strategies for Reaching the Bottom of the Pyramid," *California Management Review*, 2008.

16. Based on Nielsen Online Global Consumer Study, April 2007.

CHAPTER SIX

Marketing the Vision to the Shareholders

SHORT-TERMISM HURTS THE ECONOMY

In September 2008, Lehman Brothers collapsed.[1] The company lasted for 158 years and survived the Great Depression in the 1930s. But it did not survive the first 13 months of the modern financial crisis. It finally filed the biggest bankruptcy of all time and aggravated the worst financial crisis since the Great Depression. The fall of Lehman was just one in a series in one of the most devastating months in the history of the U.S. financial sector.[2] Fannie Mae and Freddie Mac were taken over by the government. AIG was bailed out. Washington Mutual was seized by the FDIC and Wachovia was sold.

James Collins' *How the Mighty Fall* explained this phenomenon of falling companies. It described the stages that a company experiences as it falls. Collins argued that successful companies often get arrogant and think they can do many things (stage 1), and therefore pursue aggressively wild growth (stage 2). When they find early warning signs of failure, they ignore them (stage 3), until their failure becomes very public (stage 4), and if they don't reform, they finally go bankrupt (stage 5).[3] The stages show that aggressiveness and a lack of realistic goal setting triggers the fall of companies.

Companies are often blind-sided by their eagerness to build short-term growth and ignore the risks.

In September 2009, a year after the fall of Lehman Brothers, 28 prominent figures that included Warren Buffett and Louis Gerstner signed a joint statement put together by The Aspen Institute to call for an end to short-termism in the financial markets and the creation of policies that nurture long-term value creation for shareholders and society.[4] The statement acknowledged the role of short-termism in driving risky strategies that can cause the economy to collapse. The signees agreed that long-term-driven capitalism will make a significant contribution, and they encourage shareholders to be more patient in their investments.

This short-term orientation of shareholders has also caught the attention of the government. Lord Myners, the United Kingdom's Financial Services Secretary, recently proposed a two-tier shareholding structure whereby long-term shareholders are given more votes than short-term shareholders in determining the company's strategic direction.[5] Under this system, the voting strength of short-term shareholders is restricted. Although the proposal is still under debate, many people believe that this system, which originates from family-run businesses, will help companies reduce short-term decision making.

According to Alfred Rappaport, managing earnings in the short run to meet shareholder expectations destroys shareholder value.[6] Rappaport found that most companies are trying to meet short-term shareholder expectations, even to the point of reducing value-creating long-term investments. In this chapter, we would urge companies to shift their paradigm from satisfying short-term shareholder expectations to delivering long-term corporate performance. Shareholders must go back to basics and realize that the value of a company is mostly derived from its long-term future cash flows and that the future vision will determine the performance of the company.

The definition of a company's shareholders depends on the development of the company. Kotler, Kartajaya, and Young in their book *Attracting Investors* mapped the changing nature of shareholders as a company progresses.[7] At the beginning, start-ups struggle with internal financing and bootstrapping. After a few years of operation, they might attract angels—early individual investors who use their own funds to finance start-ups with the hope of high financial reward or satisfying their interest in supporting entrepreneurship.

Later, these companies attract private equity, mostly from venture capitalists—a group of people with investment management experience and a pool of funds—that will help them realize an initial public offering (IPO). In an IPO, companies issue shares that will be publicly traded and therefore will attract a wider range of investors. The holders of the shares will have an equity stake in the company. Companies may also raise funds by issuing bonds, whereby the holders will receive regular interest payments and repayment at the time of maturity. Banks and other investors are additional sources of financing for corporations. Companies need to understand their financial shareholders in order to satisfy their needs.

A new view is emerging that the job of management is to earn a return for more than the shareholders; smart companies will focus on *all* the stakeholders—consumers, employees, channel partners, government, nonprofits, and the public at large—not just the shareholders. A successful company is never successful by itself. It is successful because it has built a superior network of stakeholders, all of whom have a stake in the business and its outcome. Satisfying the stakeholders—ensuring that they all feel rewarded—will often lead to higher long-run profitability than when the company just focuses on trying to maximize the short-run profits of the shareholders.

LONG-TERM SHAREHOLDER VALUE = VISION OF SUSTAINABILITY

We believe along with Collins and Porras that corporate vision is a result of tying corporate mission and values to the company's vision of the future.[8] The mental model of the future is the corporate vision.

We believe that the strongest future trend for corporations, especially in the capital market, is the issue of sustainability. Sustainability is a highly relevant challenge for corporations in creating shareholder value in the long run. But sustainability has two definitions. According to Kunreuther, companies view sustainability as long-term survival of the company in the business world.[9] Society, on the other hand, sees sustainability as long-term survival of the environment and social well-being. Companies have not traditionally seen the synergy between those two.

Recently, in search of new competitive advantages in the commoditized world, companies are finally becoming aware of the opportunities for achieving such a synergy. We will describe the two most important developments in recent years— market polarization and scarce resources—that lead us to this conclusion.

Polarization: Mature Market or Impoverished Market

If there is one big trend that has been bothering business-people since the end of the 1990s, it is market polarization. The market is increasingly polarized into a top and bottom end where the middle market is disappearing. In *Treasure Hunt*, Silverstein and Butman argued that their survey found middle-market consumers in the United States who earn between $50,000 and $150,000 are either trading up or trading down.[10] They either look for affordable luxuries to indulge themselves or seek bargains, or both. The authors estimate the size of trading up in the United States in 2006 to be around $500 billion while trading down is around $1 trillion. They also observed similar trends in Japan and Germany. A study of 25 industries and product categories in Europe, North America, and select additional countries by Knudsen, Randel, and Rughølm captures the same trend.[11] They found that growth in revenues from middle-market products lagged the market average by 6 percent a year from 1999 to 2004.

This has important implications for the structure of the market and how competition works. Companies have to either pursue the top-end market or pursue the low-end market. In either case, companies cannot avoid the imperative to care more about social and environmental conditions. Social and environmental conditions profoundly affect the low-end market, and this is becoming a concern of the top end of the market.

We argue that the top-end market is maturing and that high-end consumers are also becoming concerned about sustainability. When marketers decide to move up the market with top-end products, they should seriously consider the concept of sustainability. They need to touch the consumers' human spirit with a sustainable business model. Early examples of these practices are found in companies such as Whole Foods, Patagonia, and Herman Miller. They charge higher prices but maintain a very loyal consumer base that is willing to pay more for the sustainable practices of the companies.

On the other hand, a much larger consumer base is also available at the bottom end. And that is where high growth will come from in the future. Poor people are the new market opportunity, according to several experts. C.K. Prahalad and Stuart Hart are the most notable business thinkers who have been observing the potential fortune at the base of the market pyramid. Prahalad's *The Fortune at the Bottom of the Pyramid* and Hart's *Capitalism at the Crossroads* have identified the new potential of the poor as both a growing consumer market and a prominent lab for innovation.[12] Clayton Christensen even argued that disruptive technology is normally born as a solution to problems in poor society.[13] India is achieving many breakthroughs to make more products affordable to the poor. Philip Kotler and Nancy Lee, in their book *Up and Out of Poverty*, have shown how social marketing can be used to lift more people out of poverty.[14]

Poor people have been longing for some products previously not available to them not only because of income limitations but also because of access problems. Companies that want to target these consumers will need to provide solutions that overcome these barriers to consumption. Muhammad Yunus, winner of the 2008 Nobel Peace Prize, showed how banks can help poor people augment their incomes through microfinance loans.[15] Companies such as Coca-Cola, Unilever, and others are showing how they can distribute common products to more distant and isolated rural villages.[16] These solutions will also help companies in developed economies reach and serve more poor consumers.

Scarce Resources: The Earth Has a Limit

The concept of environmental sustainability in business has been evolving for the past few decades.[17] In the 1980s, as the manufacturing sector grew, the focus was to prevent and reduce pollution from manufacturing emissions. In the 1990s, when consumer-centric practices were growing, the concept was product stewardship. Companies competed to develop products that were environmentally friendly.

Today, natural resources are getting scarcer and may not support a strong growth in consumption in the long run. The prices of certain resources are soaring and increasing the cost burden for companies and ultimately customers. Companies need to conserve resources and energy to meet environmental challenges. Those that manage the scarcity of resources will be the ultimate winners. Being able to get a sustainable supply of natural resources is increasingly becoming a strong competitive advantage.

To see a company such as Whole Foods embracing the concept of environmental sustainability is no longer unusual. Whole Foods is famous for providing natural and organic products for a niche market. But when a giant company like Wal-Mart announced its move to embrace the concept in 2006, we knew that sustainability would no longer be a niche value in the business world.[18] Wal-Mart pledged to improve its productivity with more environmentally-sound practices. It also promised to buy products from more sustainable sources. It was a signal that the costs of unsustainable practices are getting higher and the only way to reduce them is by going green. It is also a warning that obtaining sustainable supply chains will soon be a major issue for corporations.

Al Gore—who won the 2007 Nobel Peace Prize and whose film on global warming, *An Inconvenient Truth,* won two Oscars—has been speaking out about the limit of earth's carrying capacity and the significant limitation it brings to the business world. He argues that the financial crisis has awakened businesspeople and alerted them to the fact that environmental sustainability will shape the future of business in the next 25 years.[19]

Environmental sustainability will also determine the progress of poverty alleviation. One can begin to appreciate the dilemma of sustainability: poverty should be alleviated but with limited resources. While trying to alleviate poverty with aggressive economic growth, governments in developing nations often ignore the preservation of the environment. Moreover, poor people are forced to deplete scarce natural resources—clean water and air and fertile agricultural soil—to maintain survival. These practices will further degrade the environment and the living conditions of the poor. The solution to these problems lies in environmentally-friendly innovations that are developed by social entrepreneurs in the impoverished area. We will discuss more about social entrepreneurship in Chapter 8.

SUSTAINABILITY AND SHAREHOLDER VALUE

The two trends—polarization and resource scarcity—will strengthen the movement toward sustainability. Companies are increasingly aware of the competitive advantage they can get if they ride the wave of sustainability. GE is a company that understands that being a values-driven business is not simply about doing good. Jeff Immelt, the CEO, recognizes sustainability as an imperative to cope with the changing business environment.[20] He realized that there is a big gap between the mature market and the growing market and closing the gap will bring good business for GE. He also argued that the economics of resource scarcity is forcing companies to create innovative solutions and GE wants to be part of the solutions. GE wants to show that it can generate profits from solving social problems, and this is already evident in its work with solar panels, wind turbines, and water quality research. As a large public company, GE views sustainable practices as a means to deliver shareholder value.

In recent years, consulting firm A.T. Kearney has found that sustainable companies have tended to outperform their peers during the financial crisis.[21] In 16 out of 18 industries examined, sustainable companies' stock prices outperformed the industry average by 15 percent from May to November 2008. Companies that practice sustainability are more resilient and adaptive to changes in the business environment. They deliver more shareholder value.

A 2008 survey of 1,254 executives around the world by the Economist Intelligence Unit also confirmed that there is a link between corporate sustainability and strong share price performance.[22] Executives from companies that emphasized reducing their social and environmental impacts reported annual profit growth of 16 percent and share price growth of 45 percent, while those from companies that did not focus on sustainability reported annual profit growth of only 7 percent and share price growth of only 12 percent.

Moreover, executives believe that the concept of sustainability is good for corporations. About 37 percent of respondents said that sustainability attracts consumers, 34 percent said sustainability improves shareholder value, and 26 percent said that it attracts good employees. Therefore, about 61 percent of the business leaders said that communicating with shareholders about their companies' performance on sustainability is a priority on their agenda over the next five years. About 24 percent of respondents said that it is their leading priority, while 37 percent said it is a major priority.

There is also growing interest in sustainability from investors. The interest drives the development of indexes that track sustainable practices. Consider the following:

- The KLD Broad Market Social Index (BSMI) defines good business practices as those that include environmental, social, and governance (ESG) consideration.[23]

- The FTSE4Good Index defines good companies as companies that work toward environmental sustainability, have positive relationships with all stakeholders, protect universal human rights, possess good supply chain labor standards, and counter bribery practices.[24]

- The Dow Jones Sustainability Index (DJSI) views sustainable business practices as a means to achieve higher profit productivity by capturing the market potential of sustainability-conscious consumers while reducing the costs and risks associated with unsustainable practices, such as costs of waste management and crisis mitigation. It defines corporate sustainability as "a business approach that creates long-term shareholder value by embracing opportunities and managing risks deriving from economic, environmental, and social developments."[25]

- Goldman Sachs has introduced the GS Sustain Focus List, which includes a list of companies with sustainable practices.[26] Aware of the fact that the world becomes increasingly transparent and growth is migrating to the BRIC countries, Goldman Sachs includes the concept of ESG similar to that of the BSMI. Moreover, the list also contains an analysis of emerging industries such as alternative energy, environmental technology, biotechnology, and nutrition as well as the practices in those industries.

In a nutshell, these indexes track companies' triple bottom lines, namely, how well a company performs in relationship to *profit*, *planet*, and *people*. It measures a company's economic, environmental, and social impact on society. David Blood, however, criticized these indexes because they fail to acknowledge that sustainability practices are an integral part of corporate strategy.[27] In developing the indexes, the team that does the sustainability research is often different from the team that does strategy research and planning. Therefore, the linkage between sustainability and strategy might sometimes be ignored.

MARKETING VISIONARY STRATEGY

According to Willard, there are three main reasons why companies choose the path of sustainable business practices.[28] One reason is that the founders have personal passion. Prominent examples include Ben Cohen and Jerry Greenfield of Ben & Jerry's, Anita and Gordon Roddick of The Body Shop, and Yvon Chouinard of Patagonia. A second reason is that companies experience a public relations crisis as a result of public backlash or activist movement. DuPont is one example of a company that started its sustainable practices because of a public relations crisis. Finally, companies can opt for sustainable practices because of regulatory pressures. Nike and Chevron were under scrutiny from regulatory bodies for some of their practices in the developing world.

However, these reasons do not guarantee continued sustainability. Founders cannot guard the business practices of their company once the company is sold. Mitigation of a public relations crisis and regulatory pressure are usually never a long-term solution. To be long-term, sustainability has to be the company's strategy arising out of its mission, vision, and values. Management needs to view sustainability as a source of competitive advantage that will set the company apart from the competition. This will be key to marketing the corporate vision to the shareholders.

Marketing to shareholders requires a different approach than marketing to consumers, employees, or channel members. Unlike consumers, shareholders are less impressed with compelling brand stories. They are also not employees who have strong bonds with the corporate culture. The number one consideration for shareholders is to make a return on their investment. Yet the shareholders are the ones responsible for guarding the sustainability of a business. They are persons and organizations that monitor business performance and make sure that corporate executives do their jobs well.

We know that touching the human spirit in the consumer and employee market is about making a difference in these people's lives. Touching the human spirit in the capital market is different. To convince shareholders about the importance of Marketing 3.0 principles, the company needs to provide tangible evidence that the practice of sustainability will improve shareholder value by creating a competitive advantage.

When shareholders think about performance, they think about profitability and returnability. Profitability is a short-term goal while returnability is a long-term goal. Companies such as Amazon.com or eBay were not profitable for the first few years of their existence. But the promise of returnability kept their shareholders from withdrawing their investments. The issue is to find linkage between sustainability, profitability, and returnability.

Marketing the vision to the shareholders requires building a sound business case. The McKinsey Global Survey of CFOs and investment professionals in 2008 showed that executives strongly believe that there is a contract between business and society and that sustainable business practices will improve shareholder value.[29]

Management has the obligation to communicate the long-term benefits of sustainability, preferably in financial terms. We compiled three important metrics that can be quantified financially. They are *improved cost productivity, higher revenue from new market opportunities*, and *higher corporate brand value*. The first metric can directly influence profitability while the last metric can influence returnability in the long run. The second metric is in the middle because it can influence both profitability and returnability.

Improved Cost Productivity

A good mission will gain support from empowered consumers. The cost will be lower because companies will benefit from the power of networks. Communities of consumers will spread good word-of-mouth reviews about the company's brand. Because customers share their satisfaction with other customers, the company's advertising costs are significantly reduced. Product development costs also will be reduced because of low-cost cocreation with consumers. Consumer empowerment also means reduced consumer cost-to-serve, as some business processes are performed by consumers themselves.

A company that demonstrates strong values will get support from employees and channel partners. Employee happiness will be high and their work productivity will be elevated. Companies will also save on hiring and retention costs. Because employees are living the values in their everyday work, the need for training is reduced and this is another cost saving. Employees perform better in their interactions with customers and this reduces the costs associated with customer complaints. Moreover, channel partners are more supportive and less likely to try to force higher channel remuneration.

With respect to the social and environmental context, sound practices also reduce costs. A study of 200 companies by Kaufmann, Reimann, Ehrgott, and Rauer revealed that companies can gain competitive advantage by adopting environmentally-responsible practices.[30] Their productivity is high. They consume fewer resources and produce less waste. A research study by Klassen of 100 Canadian firms also suggests that being green saves money.[31] The waste management and energy consumption is better controlled. The costs and risks associated with public backlash are lower. The access to raw materials is more sustainable. In low-income markets, distribution is helped by community networks. The consumers act as channels to other consumers and the marketing cost is lower. Because social and environmentally-friendly practices are well accepted by consumers, the cost of consumer acquisition is lower.

Management must make a compelling story and communicate these long-term cost savings to the shareholders. In businesses where costs are rising, higher productivity can be a significant competitive advantage. During a down business cycle, these cost savings can really determine whether a company can survive the downturn.

Higher Revenue from New Market Opportunities

Marketing 3.0 practices bring opportunities in various ways. From a corporate perspective, companies with a good mission, vision, and values can enter new markets more easily. They are more welcome. They will have the opportunity to participate in growth markets in developing countries. Governments in the developing markets will welcome corporate investment that will transform the lives of their people. These companies will also gain support from nongovernmental organizations to pursue their missions. Furthermore, such companies will be given more latitude in markets where regulations are normally tight. With sound business practices, companies will have less to worry about. The access to new markets means potential revenue and profit growth, especially because competition in these markets is lower than in other markets.

Corporations embracing sustainability will have access to both ends of the market: the mature markets and the impoverished markets. Consumers in mature markets love the concept of sustainability as it touches their human spirit. A survey by Cone revealed that despite financial tightness, 44 percent of consumers keep buying green products.[32] Approximately 35 percent of consumers even said that their interest increased after the crisis. A study by Forrester Research also confirmed that 80 percent of consumers are influenced by socially-responsible brands and 18 percent are willing to pay more for them.[33] Similarly, environmentally-responsible brands attract 73 percent of consumers and 15 percent of those consumers are willing to pay more. On the other hand, poor communities of consumers need solutions to their problems. Socially-responsible practices will deliver better solutions and win company respect.

From a marketing perspective, sustainability enables companies to target new market segments, especially the growing segments of collaborative, culturally active, and creative consumers. Sustainable practices earn consumer admiration and start consumer conversations. With a strong reputation in communities, companies can improve consumer acquisition. All these benefits contribute significantly to top line growth of corporations.

Higher Corporate Brand Value

Hatch and Schultz argue that corporate vision, together with image and culture, helps build the corporate brand.[34] The corporate brand delivers a seal of approval for any product produced by the company. The corporate brand provides protection from outside threats. When The Body Shop was challenged by a journalist who doubted the no-animal-testing practice, the company cited its corporate brand that is well-known by consumers as a symbol of no-animal-testing. The journalist's claim failed to hurt the integrity of The Body Shop.

Executives know that sustainable practices are good for the company's reputation. A BSR/Cone survey in 2008 reported that about 84 percent of professionals agree that the reputational benefit of corporate responsibility is increasingly essential.[35] But the concept of corporate reputation is intangible and therefore sometimes difficult for shareholders to accept. Fortunately, many consulting firms such as Interbrand and Brand Finance offer services to valuate corporate brand reputation and brand equity. The brand equity metrics can be interpreted financially and thus are more relevant for shareholders. Interbrand, for instance, calculated a 25 percent increase in GE's brand value as a result of its "ecoimagination" agenda—an initiative of GE to provide solutions to environmental problems.[36] This finding indicates that a commitment to sustainability can have a significant impact on the company's reputation and brand.

SUMMARY: BUSINESS CASE FOR MARKETING 3.0

To convince shareholders, a company's management needs to formulate and communicate the corporate vision in addition to its mission and values. In Marketing 3.0, the corporate vision should embrace the concept of sustainability as it will determine competitive advantage in the long run. The changes in the business landscape, particularly the market polarization and the scarce resources, contribute significantly to the increasing importance of sustainability. The company needs to communicate to its shareholders that adoption of sustainable practices will improve cost productivity, lead to higher revenue growth, and improve corporate brand value.

NOTES

1. Yalman Onaran and Christopher Scinta, "Lehman Files Biggest Bankruptcy Case as Suitors Balk," *Bloomberg*, September 15, 2008.
2. John H. Cochrane and Luigi Zingales, "Lehman and the Financial Crisis," *Wall Street Journal*, September 15, 2009.
3. Jim Collins, *How the Mighty Fall and Why Some Companies Never Give In* (New York: HarperBusiness, 2009).
4. "Overcoming Short-termism: A Call for a More Responsible Approach to Investment and Business Management." The Aspen Institute, 2009.
5. "Shareholder Rights and Wrongs," *The Economist*, August 8, 2009.
6. Alfred Rappaport, "10 Ways to Create Shareholder Value," *Harvard Business Review*, September 2006.
7. Philip Kotler, Hermawan Kartajaya, David Young, *Attracting Investors: A Marketing Approach to Finding Funds for Your Business* (Hoboken, NJ: John Wiley & Sons, 2004).

8. Jim C. Collins and Jerry I. Porras, "Organizational Vision and Visionary Organization," *California Management Review*, Fall 1991.
9. "Forging a Link between Shareholder Value and Social Good," *Knowledge@Wharton*, May 19, 2003.
10. "The Disappearing Mid-Market," *The Economist*, May 18, 2006.
11. Trond Riiber Knudsen, Andreas Randel, and Jorgen Rughølm, "The Vanishing Middle Market," *The McKinsey Quarterly*, Number 4, 2004.
12. C.K. Prahalad, *The Fortune at the Bottom of the Pyramid: Eradicating Poverty through Profits* (Philadelphia: Wharton School Publishing, 2005); Stuart L. Hart, *Capitalism at the Crossroads: The Unlimited Business Opportunities in Solving the World's Most Difficult Problems* (Philadelphia: Wharton School Publishing, 2005).
13. Clayton M. Christensen, *The Innovator's Dilemma: When New Technologies Cause Great Firms to Fail* (New York: HarperBusiness, 2000).
14. Philip Kotler and Nancy R. Lee, *Up and Out of Poverty: The Social Marketing Solution* (Philadelphia: Wharton School Publishing, 2009).
15. Muhammad Yunus, *Banker to the Poor: Micro-Lending and the Battle against World Poverty* (New York: PublicAffairs, 2007).
16. Arphita Khare, "Global Brands Making Foray in Rural India," *Regent Global Business Review*, April 2008.
17. Lynelle Preston, "Sustainability at Hewlett-Packard: From Theory to Practice," *California Management Review*, Spring 2001.
18. Marc Gunther, "The Green Machine," *Fortune*, July 31, 2006.
19. Al Gore and David Blood, "We Need Sustainable Capitalism," *Wall Street Journal*, November 5, 2008.
20. Marc Gunther, "Money and Morals at GE," *Fortune*, November 15, 2004.
21. Daniel Mahler, "Green Winners: The Performance of Sustainability-focused Companies in the Financial Crisis," A.T. Kearney, February 9, 2009.
22. "Doing Good: Business and the Sustainability Challenge," Economist Intelligence Unit, 2008.
23. KLD Broad Market Social Index Fact Sheet, KLD Research & Analytics, 2009.

24. FTSE4Good Index Series Inclusion Criteria, FTSE International Limited, 2006.
25. *Dow Jones Sustainability World Index Guide Book Version 11.1*, Dow Jones, September 2009.
26. "Introducing GS Sustain," Goldman Sach Investment Research, June 22, 2007.
27. Lenny T. Mendonca and Jeremy Oppenheim, "Investing in Sustainability: An Interview with Al Gore and David Blood," *The McKinsey Quarterly*, May 2007.
28. Bob Willard, *The Next Sustainability Wave: Building Boardroom Buy-in* (British Columbia: New Society Publishers, 2005).
29. "Valuing Corporate Social Responsibility," *The McKinsey Quarterly*, February 2009.
30. Lutz Kaufmann, Felix Reimann, Matthias Ehrgott, and Johan Rauer, "Sustainable Success: For Companies Operating in Developing Countries, It Pays to Commit to Improving Social and Environmental Conditions," *Wall Street Journal*, June 22, 2009.
31. Carol Stephenson, "Boosting the Triple Bottom Line," *Ivey Business Journal*, January/February 2008.
32. 2009 Cone Consumer Environmental Survey, Cone, 2009.
33. Sally Cohen, "Making the Case for Environmentally and Socially Responsible Consumer Products," Forrester, 2009.
34. Mary Jo Hatch and Majken Schultz, "Are the Stars Aligned for Your Corporate Brand?," *Harvard Business Review*, February 2001.
35. BSR/Cone 2008 Corporate Sustainability in a New World Survey, Cone, 2008.
36. Jez Frampton, "Acting Like a Leader: The Art of Sustainable Sustainability," Interbrand, 2009.

PART III

APPLICATION

CHAPTER SEVEN

Delivering Socio-Cultural Transformation

MARKETING TO THE POST-GROWTH MARKET

A maturing market always poses a challenge for marketers. There is little or no growth. Existing consumers are knowledgeable and begin to see products as commodities. Creative companies differentiate themselves in this market with great service and exciting experience. All of those may fuel market growth for a while but they will eventually be commodities as well. Marketers need to step up and deliver transformation.[1] Transformation lasts longer as it makes a stronger impact on human lives.

In mature markets such as the United States and the United Kingdom, an increasing number of consumers favor companies whose activities have a positive socio-cultural impact. Consider the following from recent surveys.

- For the past 15 years, surveys by Cone have consistently shown that 85 percent of American consumers have positive images of companies that support social challenges. Even in difficult times, more than half of the consumers still expect companies to support social challenges.[2]

- Even during the recession, 38 percent of Americans were undertaking socially-conscious activities in 2009.[3]

- The majority of consumers in the United Kingdom (93 percent) want companies to improve the social impact of their products and services, according to a survey by Ipsos Mori.[4]

Companies need to address the challenges in society and participate in finding solutions. In the United States, profound social issues include wellness, privacy, and job losses due to offshoring. The challenges have been around for years. Everyone knows them and yet no one would expect any corporation to be able to solve them overnight. Being a marketer in the 3.0 era is not about single-handedly creating change but about collaborating with other companies to find creative ways to solve problems.

Two forces oblige companies in a mature market to support a transformation. These are the need for future growth and the call for strong differentiation. The following two examples show why transforming consumer lifestyles can stimulate growth and create strong differentiation.

Need for Future Growth: Disney on Children's Nutrition

The Walt Disney Company primarily focuses on entertainment. Besides its theme parks, Disney is the world's biggest character franchisor—Mickey Mouse, Donald Duck, Winnie the Pooh and many others—with a comfortable lead against other well-known character owners such as Warner Bros. and Nickelodeon. Recently, Disney acquired one of its competitors, Marvel Comics, for $4 billion to strengthen its position in the character franchise market.[5]

Besides the focus on entertainment, the company also leverages its access to children by selling consumer products.

In this particular business area, it addresses consumer wellness challenges—obesity specifically—and builds the issue into its business model.[6] Disney Consumer Products (DCP) is trying to transform the eating habits of children in collaboration with several partners.

In 2004, DCP learned from a UNICEF report that over 30 percent of U.S. children between 5 and 9 years old were overweight and 14 percent were obese. DCP itself was not seen as a major contributor to this problem but was spotlighted because one of its franchisees was McDonald's, which was perceived as a key contributor to child obesity in the United States. To help in the growing health awareness among children and their moms, DCP designed a set of nutrition guidelines called "better for you" which was adapted from the guidelines set by the U.S. Food and Drug Administration (FDA). The internal guidelines outline a basic formula for Disney's franchisees to produce healthy foods. DCP applied the guidelines to Imagination Farms, its franchisee for fresh produce. It also collaborated with Kroger, one of the largest supermarket chains in the United States, to develop Disney-branded private label products based on the guidelines. Today, DCP contributes around 6 percent of the entire Disney business conglomerate's revenues and is part of the global solution for obesity.[7]

The company's move is a strategy to anticipate the emerging trends of health conscious consumers. The best strategy is to engage the future consumers: the children. Connecting with them early in their lives will help Disney capture future growth in the mature market.

Call for Strong Differentiation: Wegmans on Healthy Living

As a category killer, Wal-Mart poses a great threat to supermarkets. The only differentiation that other grocers rely on is the spatial differentiation due to their more convenient store locations. That differentiation is now relatively weak after Wal-Mart's move into neighborhood markets. Without stronger differentiation, grocers will have difficulty justifying their higher prices and competing against Wal-Mart's every-day lower prices.

To cope with this challenge, several grocers have worked to build up their differentiation and, in the process, trans-form the lifestyles of their consumers. Wegmans Food Mar-kets is one example. A privately-owned supermarket chain that promotes a healthy lifestyle, Wegmans is rated one of the best companies in *Fortune* magazine's annual survey of best companies to work for.[8] It supports its employees in develop-ing healthy lifestyles. Wegmans is also considered one of the best in merchandising and creating comprehensive in-store experiences with its supplementary pharmacy, wine shop, video rentals, dry cleaner, bookstore, and child play area. The store's retail floor productivity is above average and its oper-ating margin is better than that of Wal-Mart and even Whole Foods.

Wegmans has popularized the concept of "home meal re-placement" by providing healthy and tasty prepared foods. It promotes the "eat well, live well" principle, which is a combi-nation of eating fruits and vegetables, doing physical exercise, tracking calories, and measuring progress on a health index. Wegmans believes that health is highly correlated with nu-trition and that promoting a healthy lifestyle contributes to the community and is good for its business. Along with other grocers such as Whole Foods, the company is creating game-changing rules for the industry. As consumer health aware-ness increases, other grocers are using the issue of health as a differentiator. Even Wal-Mart is forced to address the issue of health in its marketing activities. Stronger differentiation on the part of other grocers reduces Wal-Mart's ability to be a category killer in the grocery segment.[9]

FROM PHILANTHROPY TO TRANSFORMATION

More businesses are addressing social issues through philan-thropy. Companies donate a portion of their revenues to char-ities or a specific social cause. Education is known to be the favorite object for philanthropy in which 75 percent of companies are participating.[10] Although the donations will help a good cause, many companies use philanthropy primarily to improve their reputation or get a tax deduction.

Philanthropy is not limited to the mature markets in the West. In emerging markets, philanthropy is even more popular. Merrill Lynch-Capgemini finds that Asia's millionaires committed 12 percent of their wealth for social causes, while millionaires in North America only contribute 8 percent and those in Europe 5 percent.[11]

Although philanthropy helps society, we should never overestimate its socio-cultural impact. Recent growth in philanthropy is driven by the changes in the society. People are more concerned about other people around them and are more willing to give back to society. Even in a recession, 75 percent of Americans still donate to a social cause, according to a Gallup poll.[12] But philanthropy does not stimulate transformation in the society. Transformation in the society drives philanthropy. That is why addressing social issues with philanthropic activities will have a rather short-term impact.

A more advanced form of addressing social challenges is cause marketing—a practice where companies support a specific cause through their marketing activities. The American Express Company first used cause marketing when it wanted to help raise money for the repair of the Statue of Liberty. The company said that it would donate 1 percent of the charges to its credit card to the repair fund. Many Americans responded by charging their purchases to the American Express Card instead of Visa or MasterCard.

In cause marketing, companies direct their energy, not just their money, to address the cause. They start to link the cause to their products. For example, Quaker launched a campaign against hunger as an effort to promote the health benefit of oatmeal.[13] A number of actions will be carried out including food drives, grants for social activities, and oatmeal donations. Haagen-Dazs' "Help the Honey Bee" program aims at preserving colonies of honey bees and positions honey bees as an important source of food supply, especially for making ice cream.[14] Through social media, consumers are encouraged to plant flowers and eat natural foods to help the bees. Two groceries, Waitrose in the United Kingdom and Whole Foods in the United States, are practicing cause marketing.[15] Every time consumers shop, they will be handed a token, which they can insert into any local charity box they want. At the end of the campaign, the tokens in each box will be exchanged for cash and donated to the designated charity.

Many philanthropic companies have chosen to support a specific cause that appeals to their specific consumers or employees. The Avon Corporation has helped raised over one hundred million dollars to support breast cancer research.[16] Clearly, its customers are primarily women and Avon wants to help in this cause that is primarily associated with women. Motorola is generous in supporting major engineering schools. Motorola profits from improved teaching and research in engineering schools in that they hire many engineers.[17]

Philanthropy and cause marketing have been gaining popularity in recent years. A global survey by Edelman suggests that 85 percent of consumers prefer socially responsible brands, 70 percent will pay more for the brands, and 55 percent will even recommend the brands to their family and friends.[18] Companies are aware of this fact. They are increasingly recognizing that their employees, consumers, and the public at large develop a view of a company not only based on the quality of its products and services but also on its degree of social responsibility. A majority of business executives around the world (95 percent) acknowledged that business has to contribute to society.[19] They predicted that demand from consumers and employees to support social causes will influence their strategy in the next five years.

Today, both philanthropy and cause marketing are still working but they are not used strategically. They are often only part of a public relations or marketing communications strategy. Therefore, they are not shaping the view of top-level executives and how executives run their businesses.

Corporate executives still see social causes as a responsibility instead of an opportunity to create growth and differentiation.

Another issue is that company philanthropy may lead to some consumer involvement but doesn't tend to empower or transform them. Their lifestyles stay the same. Empowerment means self-actualization. It is about allowing your consumers to move up the Maslow pyramid and fulfill their higher needs. Creating transformation is the ultimate form of marketing to the mature market.

In Marketing 3.0, addressing social challenges should not be viewed only as a tool of public relations or as a way to diffuse criticism of some negative fallout from the company's practices. On the contrary, companies should act as good corporate citizens and address social problems deeply within their business models. Some companies can strengthen their impact by moving from philanthropy and cause marketing campaigns into socio-cultural transformation (see Figure 7.1).

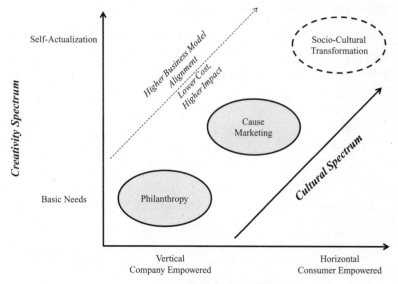

Figure 7.1   Three Stages of Addressing Social Issues in Marketing

Socio-cultural transformation sees consumers as human beings who should be empowered to move up the Maslow pyramid. It is more relevant to companies not only at the product level but also at the business model level. By utilizing the power of collaboration, it can lower cost and create higher impact.

THREE STEPS TO TRANSFORMATION

Delivering socio-cultural transformation involves a three-step process that begins with defining which challenges to address (see Figure 7.2). Once specific challenges are chosen, a company should define its key constituents who mainly include its target market and the surrounding stakeholders and community where it does business. The final step is to offer transformational solutions.

Identify Socio-Cultural Challenges

A company should choose to promote issues based on three criteria: the relevance with its vision-mission-values, the business impact, and the social impact.

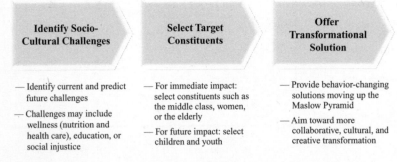

Identify Socio-Cultural Challenges	Select Target Constituents	Offer Transformational Solution
— Identify current and predict future challenges — Challenges may include wellness (nutrition and health care), education, or social injustice	— For immediate impact: select constituents such as the middle class, women, or the elderly — For future impact: select children and youth	— Provide behavior-changing solutions moving up the Maslow Pyramid — Aim toward more collaborative, cultural, and creative transformation

Figure 7.2 Three Steps of Creating Socio-Cultural Transformation

In mature markets, wellness is the one popular social cause that many companies are addressing. Health care costs in the United States have reached 16 percent of the total GDP, or $2 billion per year since 2006.[20] But the interesting fact is that the majority of the health problems are caused by bad, yet preventable, lifestyle behaviors. Around 45 percent of premature deaths are caused by obesity, unfitness, and smoking. A significant number of people in the United States are either overweight or obese. Instead of exercising regularly, they smoke. These lifestyles create serious burdens on the economy. Hence, changing the lifestyles of consumers could have a major impact not only on society's wellness but also on the economy.

Wellness itself is a broad theme that includes several sub-themes such as malnutrition, imbalanced diet, obesity, and unfitness; various kinds of disease and epidemics; natural disaster and refugees; personal and work safety; and many others. Companies that choose nutrition themes include well-known companies such as organics advocate Whole Foods and slimming advocate Subway. Themes like disease prevention and medication are the province of pharmaceutical companies such as Merck, GlaxoSmithKline, and Novartis, which are improving access to specific medicines in certain communities.

Education is also one of the most popular themes. While wellness themes are generally selected by food and beverage, grocery retail, and pharmaceutical companies, education themes are often selected by services companies. One of the prominent cause marketing programs in education is IBM's Reinventing Education. The program leverages IBM's resources (researchers, consultants, and technology) to help schools around the world in executing their educational transformation. The program has strategic importance to IBM especially in developing talents to support its future business. Another education program by IBM is the KidSmart Early Learning Program. The software and web-based program is utilized by 2.6 million children in 60 countries to enhance their learning experience.

Social justice is another popular theme and includes fair trade, employment diversity, and empowerment of women. One of the well-known companies that has chosen social justice as its key theme is The Body Shop. The values such as "support community trade" and "no animal testing" and programs such as "Stop Violence in the Home" are reflections of the company's commitment to promoting social justice. Social justice also covers the issue of offshoring. The emergence of China and India poses significant challenges in developed nations. As companies pursue efficiency and move offshore, many people lose their jobs and the economy may potentially be hurt.[21]

Privacy is another issue. The rise of consumer-centricity, especially the one-to-one marketing in the last few years, spurs the use of data mining tools. Consumers are dynamically profiled every time they use their loyalty card or credit card. In pursuit of behavioral insights, consumers are ethnographically videotaped with surveillance cameras in retail stores. Social media and Google searches may reveal identities of consumers publicly. This is a dilemma in Marketing 3.0: as consumers are increasingly networked, they have no personal space. IBM, together with vendors from Eclipse Group, tries to solve this social challenge with the Higgins project.[22] Higgins will allow consumers to browse the Internet without the fear of losing their privacy. It will mask consumers' personal identities while active on their networks.

Select Target Constituents

The selection of target constituents also requires understanding a company's key stakeholders—especially the consumers, employees, distributors, dealers, suppliers, and public at large. To make a significant impact, companies should choose constituents that have major influence in the overall society.

There are typically three types of constituents. Gender and age groups such as women, youth, and the elderly are the first. Women are often underestimated for their potential. In the book *Don't Think Pink*, the authors point out that a large number of women not only contribute half of the household income and own businesses but also act as purchasing agents in the home and in the office.[23] Silverstein and Sayre argue that women will drive the economy due to their purchasing power ($13 trillion in annual income), which is more than twice the combined GDP forecast of China and India in 2009.[24] Women also hold the decision making power when it comes to important issues such as food and fitness. These two issues are the major roots of many social problems related to health care. Moreover, consumer empowerment will work better for women than for men. Some 44 percent of women do not feel empowered and therefore seek out empowering brands.

Targeting the oldest and the youngest members of the society —the baby boomers and Gen Y—will give companies an opportunity to make an impact as well. A survey by the Hidden Brain Drain Task Force as well as the complementary focus groups and interviews conducted by Hewlett, Sherbin, and Sumberg revealed this fact.[25] Both the top and bottom age segments love to contribute to society (86 percent of Gen Y and 85 percent of baby boomers) even more than the segments between them.

Youth are more aware of social issues according to a poll by Youthography. About 90 percent of American youth consider social responsibility important in their purchase decisions. Moreover, children and youth are considered the future consumers. For that reason, they are typically a key constituent for nutrition and education. In countries with aging populations such as Japan and most countries in Europe, the elderly are considered a primary target market for health products and services.[26] In many cases, they could become the key constituents for social justice and disease prevention.

The second type of constituent is the middle-class group. Persons in the middle class are not poor but have limited resources. Eduardo Giannetti da Fonseca, a distinguished Brazilian economist, defines the middle class as "people who are not resigned to a life of poverty, who are prepared to make sacrifices to create a better life for themselves but who have not started with life's material problems solved because they have material assets to make their lives easy."[27] The middle class is the biggest consumer market, but people in the group have major challenges with wellness, education, and social justice. Therefore, addressing such themes may attract the middle class as key constituents.

The third type of constituent are minority groups. This segment includes certain races, religious believers, and the disabled who lack empowerment in society. The group is most often a constituent for the diversity cause. *Fortune* magazine annually ranks 100 best companies to work in for minorities. The magazine's 2009 list of the most diverse employers includes companies such as Four Seasons Hotel, Qualcomm, T-Mobile, and Cisco Systems which have more than 40 percent minority employees.

Offer Transformational Solution

The final step is to provide the transformational solutions. A survey by McKinsey revealed that companies are expected to solve social challenges by creating jobs (65 percent), developing breakthrough innovation (43 percent), and making products or services that provide solutions to the issues (41 percent).[28]

Office Depot, for instance, tries to help society by creating jobs by doing business with small vendors from historically underutilized businesses or HUBs.[29] Office Depot is also inspired by the local hiring practices of one of its vendors, Master Manufacturing, a company that produces chair casters and cushions. The company creates jobs for minorities and it has become one of its key differentiations. Office Depot, by collaborating with HUBs, gains competitive advantage and demand for their products is high. More importantly, it creates local jobs as a way to combat the issue of offshoring.

Breakthrough innovations aim at moving human beings up the Maslow Pyramid. IDEO, a design company, creates an innovative approach called the Human-Centered Design.[30] It views solutions through three lenses: desirability (how deep is the need for the solution), feasibility (how possible is it to execute technically and organizationally), and viability (how promising is it from a financial perspective).

Companies can adopt this open-source approach by conducting a three-phase process: hear, create, and deliver. In the hear phase, a team of multidisciplinary people will do the deep dive, ethnographic research done to reveal hidden challenges in detail. The team will immerse itself in select communities and capture stories and metaphors and try to understand the human needs of the target constituents. In the create phase, they will identify opportunities, design solutions, and develop prototypes through synthesis and brainstorming. The team will assess the desirability through feedback loops. Finally, in the deliver phase, they will do feasibility and viability assessment and develop the plans.

Remember that companies are not expected to do the transformation alone. They have to collaborate with one another and with the stakeholders. In fact, they must collaborate with their competitors. Whole Foods and Wegmans, for instance, are essentially competitors. But together they stimulate a giant competitor like Wal-Mart to advocate healthy living. All three of them are cocreating transformation in the society.

SUMMARY: BUILDING TRANSFORMATION INTO YOUR COMPANY'S CHARACTER

Companies are traditionally started for the purpose of making a profit through satisfying some set of market wants and desires. If they succeed and grow, they will usually receive requests to make donations to worthwhile causes. They may handle this by giving miscellaneous small contributions or by establishing cause marketing campaigns.

Over time, then, the public begins to expect companies to operate as engines for socio-cultural development and not engines for profit making. An increasing number of consumers might begin to judge companies in part by their level of commitment to public and social issues. Some companies may rise to the occasion by building social challenge into the very fabric of their character. They transform the society. At that point, such companies have entered the Marketing 3.0 stage of being.

NOTES

1. B. Joseph Pine II and James H. Gilmore, *The Experience Economy: Work Is Theater and Every Business a Stage* (Boston: Harvard Business Press, 1999).
2. The 2008 Cone Cause Evolution Study, Cone, 2008.
3. Richard Stengel, "Doing Well by Doing Good," *Time*, September 10, 2009.
4. Liza Ramrayka, "The Rise and Rise of the Ethical Consumer," *Guardian*, November 6, 2006.
5. Ryan Nakashima, "Disney to Purchase Marvel Comics for $4B," *Time*, August 31, 2009.
6. David E. Bell and Laura Winig, "Disney Consumer Products: Marketing Nutrition to Children," Harvard Business School Case, 2007.
7. Based on the 2007 and 2008 figures, *The Walt Disney Fact Book*, 2008.
8. Matthew Boyle, "The Wegmans Way," *Fortune*, January 24, 2005.
9. Mark Tatge, "As a Grocer, Wal-Mart is No Category Killer," *Forbes*, June 30, 2003.
10. "The State of Corporate Philanthropy: A McKinsey Global Survey," *The McKinsey Quarterly*, January 2008.

11. Survey by Merrill Lynch and Capgemini, cited in Shu-Ching Jean Chen, "When Asia's Millionaires Splurge, They Go Big," *Fortune*, 2007.

12. Gallup Poll, December 19, 2008.

13. Emily Bryson York, "Quaker Kicks Off Brand Campaign in Times Square," *Advertising Age*, March 9, 2009.

14. Karen Egolf, "Haagen-Dazs Extends Its Honey-Bee Efforts," *Advertising Age*, August 4, 2009.

15. "Shoppers Determine Grocers' Charitable Giving," *RetailWire*, September 5, 2008.

16. Ron Irwin, "Can Branding Save the World?" *Brandchannel*, April 8, 2002.

17. "Motorola Foundation Grants $5 Million to Programs that Engage Budding Innovators," press release, Motorola, June 25, 2009.

18. Survey by Edelman, Edelman press release, November 15, 2007, cited in Ryan McConnell, "Edelman: Consumers Will Pay Up to Support Socially Conscious Marketers," *Advertising Age*, November 16, 2007.

19. Debby Bielak, Sheila M.J. Bonini, and Jeremy M. Oppenheim, "CEOs on Strategy and Social Issues," *The McKinsey Quarterly*, October 2007.

20. Brendan C. Buescher and Paul D. Mango, "Innovation in Health Care: An Interview with the CEO of the Cleveland Clinic," *The McKinsey Quarterly*, March 2008.

21. Michael Mandel, "The Real Cost of Offshoring," *BusinessWeek*, June 18, 2007.

22. Lew McCreary, "What Was Privacy," *Harvard Business Review*, October 2008.

23. Lisa Johnson and Andrea Learned, *Don't Think Pink: What Really Makes Women Buy—and How to Increase Your Share of This Crucial Market* (New York: AMACOM, 2004).

24. Michael J. Silverstein and Kate Sayre, "The Female Economy," *Harvard Business Review*, September 2009

25. Sylvia Ann Hewlett, Laura Sherbin, and Karen Sumberg, "How Gen Y & Boomers Will Reshape Your Agenda," *Harvard Business Review*, July–August 2009.

26. Ian Rowley and Hiroko Tashiro, "Japan: Design for the Elderly," *BusinessWeek*, May 6, 2008.

27. "Burgeoning Bourgeoisie," *The Economist*, February 12, 2009.

28. Sheila Bonini, Jieh Greeney, and Lenny Mendonca, "Assessing the Impact of Societal Issues: A McKinsey Global Survey," *The McKinsey Quarterly*, November 2007.

29. Tim Sanders, "Social Responsibility Is Dead," *Advertising Age*, September 17, 2009.

30. Human-Centered Design: An Introduction, *IDEO*, 2009.

CHAPTER EIGHT

Creating Emerging Market Entrepreneurs

FROM PYRAMID TO DIAMOND, FROM AID TO ENTREPRENEURSHIP

Lasting peace cannot be achieved unless large population groups find ways in which to break out of poverty. Microcredit is one such means. Development from below also serves to advance democracy and human rights.

—Ole Danbolt Mjøs[1]

This statement from the chairman of the Norwegian Nobel Committee led Grameen Bank, Bangladesh's microfinance institution and its founder, Muhammad Yunus, to be the cowinners of the 2006 Nobel Peace Prize. The award was an important milestone in the world's effort to reduce poverty, as stated in the United Nation's Millennium Development Goals.

Eradicating poverty is arguably humankind's biggest challenge.[2] The challenge is to transform the structure of wealth in the community from a pyramid to a diamond. A pyramid means there are a few people who have very high purchasing power at the top of the pyramid. More consumers will be at the medium section of the pyramid and the

137

majority of consumers at the very bottom.[3] The pyramid must be reshaped into a diamond. In other words, more people at the bottom of the pyramid should have higher purchasing power and therefore move to the middle level. The bottom of the pyramid will shrink and the middle will fatten.

This has been happening dramatically in China as its economy grows at a fast rate and becomes a world power. Fareed Zakaria found that poverty alleviation is happening at a faster rate in China than in any other country.[4] This is also happening in India. Extreme poverty in rural India has declined greatly from 94 percent to 61 percent in 20 years from 1985 to 2005. It is projected to decline further to 26 percent by 2025.[5] According to McKinsey Global Institute, there are five income segments in India (see Table 8.1). In 2005, the biggest disposable income belonged to the bottom segments. However, in 2025, the biggest disposable income will belong to the middle segments. As the middle segment grows, people in this group will have a different lifestyle, and discretionary spending on such items as mobile phones and personal care will climb up on their priority lists.

A team of experts led by Jeffrey Sachs predicted that this transformation from pyramid to diamond would happen universally around the world. They estimated that extreme poverty—people living on less than $1 per day—will be eliminated by the year 2025.[6] But an unlikely premise must be

Table 8.1 Prospective View of the Five Income Segments in India

No.	Segment	Annual Income (in Indian rupees)	Aggregate Disposable Income (trillion Indian rupees)		
			2005	2015	2025
1	Global	>1,000,000	2	6.3	21.7
2	Strivers	500,000 – 1,000,000	1.6	3.8	20.9
3	Seekers	200,000 – 499,999	3.1	15.2	30.6
4	Aspirers	90,000 – 199,999	11.4	14.5	13.7
5	Deprived	<90,000	5.4	3.8	2.6

fulfilled: All 22 advanced countries have agreed to provide 0.7 percent of their national income and must consistently contribute this amount of aid.[7]

However, we do not see foreign aid as a sustainable solution. It is like feeding the impoverished people fish but not teaching them how to fish. The real solution has to be an investment and a promotion of entrepreneurship. The poor should be empowered to be able to lift themselves to the middle of the pyramid.

A key actor in this solution is not nonprofits and government. It is corporations that generate the vast majority of the economic development and that own the business network. Companies should help the poor even if only for the selfish reason of expanding the market. However, ultimately the three parties have to work together in collaboration to get the job done.

THREE ENABLING FORCES AND FOUR REQUIREMENTS

Three enabling forces can make this solution happen. The first force is increased access among the poor to information and communication technology infrastructure. The impoverished community needs to be more exposed to information and income-generating opportunities. The Internet transforms farmers in India into a community of e-farmers with access to daily prices of crops in overseas trade markets. They can also search for other important information including the latest farming methods and weather forecasts. This enables them to ask for the best price for their produce.[8] The introduction of mobile phones by Grameen Phone in Bangladesh also enhances interconnectivity among farmers and hence facilitates community conversation.[9]

The next force is the blend of excess supply, underconsumption in mature markets, and hypercompetition at the top and middle of the pyramid. It stimulates companies to look for other growth markets. Banks started to serve the previously "unbankable" and provide microloans to low-income communities. Some financial institutions in Latin America, forced by the narrower spread in the top and middle markets, pursue this strategy to gain more diversified portfolio risk.[10] Multinational companies such as Unilever have established a foothold in the rural market in search of growth.[11] These consumers have simple needs and therefore require a lower cost to serve. Dell is embracing the Indian market with affordable computers to compensate for its declining sales in mature markets and is collaborating with a number of channel partners.[12]

The final force is government policy to discourage people from migrating to overcrowded urban areas. Urban growth will put heavy pressure on the urban infrastructure. Investment in the rural areas, on the other hand, will increase the quality of life of the rural people and help slow migration. This is what China was aiming at when it planned to increase its budget for investment in rural areas by more than USD13.9 billion in 2008.[13] It is a strategic step to avoid the kind of infrastructure impairment that happens in India where growth is heavily concentrated in megacities such as Delhi, Mumbai, and Calcutta.[14]

All three forces help deliver a huge underserved market. Ease of information access makes it easier to promote products and educate the market. And governments will want to support and facilitate any companies that would like to invest in rural development.

Our observation of these three forces leads us to a solid conclusion: doing well by doing good disruptively—having impressive business growth by making poverty history—can be achieved by investing in emerging markets or in the low end of an established market. This is what Stuart Hart and Clayton Christensen referred to as a "great leap downward"—to the bottom of the economic pyramid, where disruptive innovation is needed to address the social challenges caused by the imbalanced economic growth.[15] Disruptive innovation usually brings cheaper, simpler, and more convenient products that are initially embraced by poor consumers.[16] Examples of disruptive innovations for the poor would include a cell phone selling for $5, a laptop selling for $100, and so on.

However, to ensure that the disruptive innovation truly reduces poverty, Michael Chu put forward four requirements:[17]

1. Its scale should be huge to reach the billions who are in poverty.
2. Solutions must be enduring and last over generations.
3. Solutions must be truly effective and make a difference.
4. All this must happen efficiently.

Grameen Danone Foods in Bangladesh is one of the few companies that understands these four requirements. When Grameen Group and Groupe Danone formed the 50-50 joint venture, the mission they had in mind was simple: saving the world with a cup of yogurt.[18] An affordable dairy product from the company created several hundred livestock-farming and distribution jobs in the local community. Learning from this small success, the joint venture started to get ambitious. In order to address poverty in a significant way, Grameen and Danone intend to reinvest the profits of Grameen Danone Foods and expand the model throughout the country.[19] This action is 1) huge in scale because of its national rollout, 2) enduring for generations because of its job-creating impact, 3) proven effective because it creates better living conditions, and 4) efficient because it involves the community.

THE MEANING OF SOCIAL BUSINESS ENTERPRISE

Social business enterprise (SBE) is a term coined by Muhammad Yunus to describe a company that is making money while impacting the society in which it operates. It is neither an NGO nor a philanthropic foundation. An SBE is built with a social purpose in mind right from the beginning. But it is also possible to transform an established company into an SBE. The basic factor determining whether a company is dubbed an SBE will be whether the social goal remains its primary business objective and is clearly reflected in its decisions.[20]

SBEs offer the greatest hope if they can be created from the bottom of the pyramid. Indonesia—a country that is regarded as a microfinance flagship coped with the financial crisis of the 1990s and has continued to develop favorably in its aftermath—provides an interesting case. Bank Rakyat Indonesia's microfinance operations reach approximately one third of Indonesian households. It is estimated to be the world's largest microfinance institution with over 30 million savers and the third largest microcredit provider with more than 3 million borrowers.[21] The borrowers hopefully will become new social entrepreneurs who will strengthen the economic foundation of Indonesian society.

There are three measures of the success of an SBE in relation to strengthening the economic foundation of the society.[22] Using these measures, you can easily identify which company is an SBE and which is not. First, an SBE stretches disposable income. Second, it expands disposable income. And finally, it increases disposable income.

Stretches Disposable Income

An SBE stretches disposable income by providing goods and services at lower prices. An example is Unilever's Annapurna affordable iodized salt. Before the product was widely available, 30 percent of children under five in Africa had iodine deficiency disorders because of heavy consumption of cheaper noniodized salt.[23] Another example is the House-for-Life program.[24] Launched in 2005, it is a program from Holcim Sri Lanka offering low-cost housing solutions.

Expands Disposable Income

An SBE expands disposable income by providing goods and services not previously available for the bottom of the pyramid. The development of no-frills high-tech products that address the digital divide provides a good example of expanding disposable income. Nicholas Negroponte's XO and Nova netPC, the most popular efforts to provide the poor with personal computers, are examples.[25] Pharmaceutical companies such as GlaxoSmithKline and Novo Nordisk have begun to improve access to essential medicines to the bottom of the pyramid.[26]

Increases Disposable Income

An SBE increases disposable income by growing the economic activity of the underserved society. Grameen Phone illustrates an SBE by this measure. The mobile phone industry in Bangladesh—largely driven by Grameen Phone—created a total value added of $812 million in 2005 and contributed directly and indirectly to more than 250,000 income opportunities.[27] Another example is Hindustan Lever's Project Shakti, which employs thousands of underprivileged women as its sales force to bring its products to rural consumers and provides them with significant disposable income.[28] The women sell its products, which are in the form of small, affordable sachets suited to the local needs and income level. Hindustan Lever supports the entrepreneurs by providing on-the-job training and introducing them to selling skills.

To whatever level an SBE aspires, ensuring success involves a few guiding principles.

- **Market Education** SBEs must educate the underserved market continuously, not only on product benefits but also on how to increase their quality of life as related to the SBE's business. For example, an SBE selling affordable health supplements will also educate its customers about health and hygiene. Otherwise, the products will not be connected to the customers.
- **Linkage with Local Communities and the Informal Leaders** SBEs must also build linkages with local communities and the informal leaders such as doctors, teachers, heads of villages, and religious leaders. It is

very crucial in doing business with the low-income segment to eliminate the cultural barriers and resistances.

- **Partnership with the Government and NGOs** SBEs
  must partner with the government and NGOs. Linking
  the corporate objectives with the government's mission
  will help reduce the cost of market education and the
  overall campaign. Also, it will add credibility and facilitate acceptance of the SBE's effort.

MARKETING FOR POVERTY ALLEVIATION

To succeed, all marketing mix variables of an SBE may
have to be redesigned. This redesign often creates superior
and streamlined business models that challenge conventional
ones.[29] Table 8.2 provides a summary of the marketing model
that needs to be built for a social business enterprise.

Table 8.2 The Marketing Model of an SBE

No	Elements of Marketing	Social Business Enterprise Business Model
1	Segmentation	Bottom of the Pyramid
2	Targeting	High Volume Communities
3	Positioning	Social Business Enterprise
4	Differentiation	Social Entrepreneurship
5	Marketing Mix	
	• Product	Products not Currently Accessible for Low-Income Customers
	• Price	Affordable
	• Promotion	Word-of-Mouth
	• Place	Community Distribution
6	Selling	Sales Force of Social Entrepreneurs
7	Brand	Iconic
8	Service	No-Frills
9	Process	Low-Cost

Segmentation and Targeting

An SBE usually has a simple segmentation target, namely, people at the bottom of the pyramid. However, an SBE can view the market creatively by understanding the variance in attitudes of low-income consumers. Modifying the VALS system, low-income consumers can be classified into four segments[30]:

1. **Believers** Believers are conservative consumers with strong beliefs in traditional moral values. They love their families and communities. Their consumption pattern is predictable because they always choose familiar brands. Their loyalty to certain brands is high.

2. **Strivers** This type of consumer is driven by social approval. They pursue achievement to impress their peers. They choose products that they can show off and mimic those of the rich. Although achievement-driven, lack of resources inhibits them from moving forward.

3. **Makers** Makers like to express themselves through concrete activities. They build houses and farms with their practical skills. They prefer practical and functional products and are not impressed with emotional value.

4. **Survivors** Because their material resources are the lowest of the four segments, survivors focus on meeting basic needs rather than fulfilling desires. They are cautious consumers who will always look for bargains.

Because an SBE targets a segment that does not have a high value in terms of individual transactions, the aim is high-volume communities. Community is an important part of a strategy to serve lower income customers. First, it helps in spreading the word, which is important for market education and commercial communication. Second, it is easier to control the community groups. In several cases where collection of payment for the services is an issue, having a community approach is beneficial for an SBE. The community will try to safeguard its integrity and try to help its members in fulfilling their payment obligations. This is true in most microloan contexts.

Positioning-Differentiation-Brand

Poor consumers are not necessarily attracted to whatever is low cost; they value trusted brands. Therefore, the brand should be an icon of the society. According to Douglas Holt, icons represent a particular kind of story that consumers use to address their anxieties and desires.[31] In this case the anxieties and desires of the poor are the opportunity to improve their way of life.

The positioning in the target segment can be crafted in numerous ways. The company can be positioned as "a hero for the poor" or as a company that "teaches people how to fish instead of giving them free fish." The main message is the same: A social business enterprise helps people to improve their lives by providing affordable products and income-generating opportunities.

If it is a multinational company, the positioning should be localized to the community level. Philips in India, for example, positions itself as a "health care services provider for rural communities."[32] Philips India introduced DISHA (Distance Healthcare Advancement Project) in 2005 with the goal of enhancing the quality and affordability of health-care services for poor people. Philips provided mobile clinics in which poor communities can get diagnostic testing and consultation with doctors on topics such as mother-child care and trauma treatments.

To strengthen the positioning, an SBE should try to create social entrepreneurship as a differentiator. A typical differentiation for a real SBE as opposed to other socially responsible companies and NGOs is that an SBE provides a long-term solution by providing entrepreneurship at the bottom of the pyramid.

For example, the Co-operative Group in the U.K. has a set of differentiators deeply rooted in social business entrepreneurship.[33] It establishes its strong position as a leader for fair trade. Compared to other retailers, it sells more fair trade products in more stores. It has private labels of coffee dedicated to fair trade. Furthermore, with its Community Dividend scheme, customers can instantly donate their money to community causes.

Marketing Mix and Selling

A company's differentiation should be reflected in its marketing mix. Its products should be ones not currently available for low-income customers. The price should be affordable. Remember that the most important thing for low-income customers is affordability, not simply cheaper prices. D'Andrea and Herrero argued that in the context of poverty, price is associated with the Total Purchasing Cost, not just price alone.[34] Some poor customers, especially those in rural areas, often buy products in urban areas; Total Purchasing Cost can include transportation costs and other costs such as commuting time.

Companies should be creative in packaging. The strategy is the unbundling of product. When disposable incomes limit the amount consumers can buy at any one time, it becomes extremely important to deliver products and services in affordable packages. For example, companies can sell sachets as single packages for one-time use only. Companies can also create a smaller sized product package that is more affordable to lower income customers. These are called economical packages. The actual per-item price for these smaller packages is higher, but they are affordable.

Promotion will use the power of word of mouth within a community. The best way is to approach the informal leaders in the community. An informal leader can be a teacher or a religious leader. Women can also be great product ambassadors. Muhammad Yunus of Grameen Bank extends microloans virtually only to women because they are influential and they are the majority of the underserved poor. They talk to each other and create conversation in the community.

Distribution is also most effectively done on a peer-to-peer basis within a community. Traditional delivery is too costly to reach distant locations with relatively small markets. Therefore, community distribution that uses consumers as licensed sales agents in low-income areas is often the best possible solution. People trade with their own community, which creates a win-win relationship within the community itself. The buyers can consume an affordable product while the sales agents can create income for themselves.

Production and distribution costs made it unprofitable to sell physical top-up cards for mobile phones in the Philippines that are worth less than 300 pesos. Globe Telecom responded by establishing over-the-air reloading; customers pay a licensed individual distributor to top up electronically. This example also shows how the selling effort can leverage the power of community networks. Our sales force should be from our own target market. People who are in the community are best able to understand the purchase and usage behavior of their peers.

Service and Process

Because the profit margin in terms of percentage for the business at the bottom of the pyramid is relatively small, the business models should be no frills and low cost. To achieve such low cost, community-based service and process are required. Informal leaders such as school principals, teachers, and religious leaders are in the best position to serve the local communities of consumers.[35] They are the community service agents that have the information and ability to monitor the service level. Manila Water utilizes collective billing to enforce timely payment. Cemex's Patrimonio Hoy promotes its low-cost building program through teachers and church leaders to gain more buy-in from the community.

SUMMARY: ALLEVIATING POVERTY BY ENCOURAGING ENTREPRENEURSHIP

Poverty remains one of the most urgent problems facing mankind. In too many societies, the distribution of income is in the shape of a pyramid rather than a diamond, with too many poor at the base of the pyramid. But as Prahalad and others have pointed out, there is a fortune at the bottom of the pyramid. China and India, in particular, are making strong moves to turn their pyramids into diamonds. One answer is microlending to the poor, typically women, who use the money in a productive way and show very high rates of repayment. A broader answer is to encourage the formation of social business enterprises among entrepreneurs, companies, and the poor. An SBE is wedded to a social purpose but also hopes to make money in the process. SBEs offer the promise of rescuing poor people by giving them opportunities and also by using a modified marketing mix that makes their product and service offerings more affordable and accessible to the poor.

NOTES

1. Press release: Nobel Peace Prize 2006, Oslo, October 13, 2006.
2. Ethan B. Kapstein, *Economic Justice: Towards a Level Playing Field in an Unfair World* (Princeton: Princeton University Press, 2006).
3. C.K. Prahalad, *The Fortune at the Bottom of the Pyramid: Eradicating Poverty through Profits* (Philadelphia: Wharton School Publishing, 2005).
4. Fareed Zakaria, *Post-American World* (New York: W.W. Norton & Co., 2008).
5. Eric D. Beinhocker, Diana Farrell, and Adil S. Zainulbhai, "Tracking the Growth of India's Middle Class," *The McKinsey Quarterly*, August 2007.
6. Jeffrey D. Sachs, *The End of Poverty: Economic Possibilities for Our Time* (New York: Penguin Press, 2005).
7. U.N. Millennium Project 2005, Investing in Development: A Practical Plan to Achieve the Millennium Development Goals: Overview, United Nations Development Program, 2005.

8. From ITC's web site, www.itcportal.com/rural-development/echoupal.htm.

9. Ruma Paul, "Bangladesh Grameenphone Eyes Rural Users with New Plan," *Reuters*, December 1, 2008.

10. Luis Alberto Moreno, "Extending Financial Services to Latin America's Poor," *The McKinsey Quarterly*, March 2007.

11. From Unilever's web site, www.unilever.com/sustainability/.

12. "Dell Eyes $1 Billion Market in India," *The Financial Express*, August 13, 2008.

13. "China to Increase Investment in Rural Areas by over 100 Billion Yuan," *People' Daily*, January 31, 2008.

14. Patrick Barta and Krishna Pokharel, "Megacities Threaten to Choke India," *Wall Street Journal*, May 13, 2009.

15. Stuart L. Hart, *Capitalism at the Crossroads: The Unlimited Business Opportunities in Solving the World's Most Difficult Problems* (Philadelphia: Wharton School Publishing, 2005).

16. Clayton M. Christensen, *The Innovator's Dilemma: When New Technologies Cause Great Firms to Fail* (New York: HarperBusiness, 2000).

17. Garry Emmons, "The Business of Global Poverty: Interview with Michael Chu," Harvard Business School Working Knowledge, April 4, 2007.

18. Sheridan Prasso, "Saving the World with a Cup of Yogurt," *Fortune*, March 15, 2007.

19. Press release—Danone, "Launching of Danone Foods Social Business Enterprise," March 16, 2006.

20. Muhammad Yunus, "Social Business Entrepreneurs Are the Solution," www.grameen-info.org/bank/socialbusiness entrepreneurs.htm.(last modified August 20, 2005, last accessed May 2, 2007).

21. Don Johnston, Jr. and Jonathan Morduch, "The Unbanked: Evidence from Indonesia," *The World Bank Economic Review*, 2008.

22. Michael Chu, "Commercial Returns and Social Value: The Case of Microfinance," Harvard Business School Conference on Global Poverty, December 2, 2005.

23. From Unilever's web site: www.unilever.com/sustainability/casestudies/health-nutrition-hygiene/globalpartnershipwith unicef.aspx.

24. From Holcim's web site www.holcim.com/CORP/EN/id/1610640158/mod/7_2_5_0/page/ case_study.html.

25. Steve Hamm, "The Face of the $100 Laptop," *BusinessWeek*, March 1, 2007.
26. Farhad Riahi, "Pharma's Emerging Opportunity," *The McKinsey Quarterly*, September 2004.
27. Nicholas P. Sullivan, *You Can Hear Me Now: How Microloans and Cell Phones Are Connecting the World's Poor to the Global Economy* (San Francisco, Jossey-Bass, 2007).
28. "Marketing to Rural India: Making the Ends Meet," *India Knowledge@Wharton*, March 8, 2007.
29. Kunal Sinha, John Goodman, Ajay S. Moorkerjee, and John A. Quelch, "Marketing Programs to Reach India's Underserved," in V. Kasturi Rangan, John A. Quelch, Gustavo Herrero, and Brooke Barton (editors), *Business Solutions for the Global Poor: Creating Social and Economic Value* (San Francisco: Jossey-Bass, 2007).
30. VALS is the system that identifies current and future opportunities by segmenting the consumer marketplace on the basis of the personality traits that drive consumer behavior. See www.sric-bi.com/VALS/ for more detailed description of the segmentation.
31. Douglas B. Holt, *How Brands Become Icons: The Principles of Cultural Branding* (Boston: Harvard Business School Press, 2004).
32. Cécile Churet & Amanda Oliver, *Business for Development*, World Business Council for Sustainable Development, 2005.
33. From the Co-operative Group's web site: www.co-operative.coop/.
34. Guillermo D'Andrea and Gustavo Herrero, "Understanding Consumers and Retailers at the Base of the Pyramid in Latin America," Harvard Business School Conference on Global Poverty, December 2, 2005.
35. Christopher P. Beshouri, "A Grassroots Approach to Emerging Market Consumers," *The McKinsey Quarterly*, 2006, Number 4.

CHAPTER NINE

Striving for Environmental Sustainability

Another way to make a difference is to solve one of the biggest global issues of our times: environmental sustainability. Many companies have not started to think seriously about making their processes friendlier to the environment. Some companies felt the pressure and scrutiny and knew they had to do something before being spotted and publicly embarrassed by environmentalists. At the other end were a few companies that felt that they could take advantage of this public interest by aggressively marketing green-related products and services.

THE THREE ACTORS IN SUSTAINING THE ENVIRONMENT

We will present three cases of larger companies that have created big impacts on the environment—albeit each in different ways. From these three cases—DuPont, Wal-Mart, and Timberland—we can distinguish three roles that companies can adopt to protect Mother Nature—the Innovator, the Investor, or the Propagator.

The Innovator: DuPont Case

DuPont, the science company that has existed for more than two centuries, has dramatically transformed itself from being the worst U.S. polluter to one of its greenest corporations today.[1] The inventor of nylon, Dacron, Lucite, Kevlar, Corian, Tyvek, Teflon, and polymer chemistry that would change human lives forever was also the creator of chlorofluorocarbon (CFC) to which the hole in the ozone layer above Antarctica can be attributed. However, today, the company is one of the main drivers of the U.S. Climate Action Partnership (USCAP), which has requested legislation that obliges corporations to apply lower-cost methods that will reduce the greenhouse gas emissions of their businesses. Within DuPont itself, gas emissions have been reduced by 72 percent from 1990 to 2003 and the goal is for a further reduction of 15 percent by 2015.

In addition to its pollution reduction success, DuPont is integrating sustainability as both its operations obligation and its core business model. What is most inspiring is that $5 billion of its $29 billion in revenue comes from sustainable products: products made from environmentally-friendly sources and products that save energy. DuPont has ingrained the mission not only to slow down environmental problems by addressing harmful operations within the company but also to create products that will stop further harm from being done to the planet. As noted by one of DuPont's executives, "My team knows that when they walk into my office with an idea about a new product, it'd better have a reduced environmental footprint, or they can walk right out. Because [if it doesn't] I'm not listening!"

DuPont is an example of the environmental Innovator. The Innovator invents/innovates products that have the potential to save the environment, not products that simply do not harm nature and are environmental-friendly. These products reverse the damage done and do not damage the environment in either their production process or in their disposal.

Innovators go beyond incremental innovation to develop disruptive innovation. Hart and Milstein label incremental innovation as an attribute in strategies for greening and disruptive or discontinuous innovation as a component in strategies for beyond greening.[2]

DuPont illustrates the Innovator's role because of its constant exploration of technologies to create new and better products. It constantly repositions itself to align with the changing needs and themes of the world. When the power of nations was once defined by guns and weapons in the early 1800s, DuPont was a gunpowder and explosives manufacturer. And then in the late 1800s, when war began to incorporate biological warfare and the strongest country possessed the best scientists and discoveries, DuPont transformed itself into a chemical company producing synthetic materials. A century and more later when global warming and cries from environmentalists set in, DuPont underwent its second drastic transformation to become a company that focuses on sustainability by producing energy-saving products.

DuPont has created several products that may potentially reverse some damage done to the environment. One of its products, Tyvek, can be used in new ways to improve energy efficiency. DuPont's biofuel unit is working to make corn yield more ethanol, finding a cheaper way to produce higher-energy cellulosic ethanol, and partnering with BP on a new fuel called bio-butanol, a high-energy fuel that works in today's engines. The company has also applied Kevlar, the substance used for bulletproof vests, in fuel-efficient planes.

The Innovator has the scientific capability to contribute to the environment in a way that the Investor or Propagator lack. The innovations produce major impacts on the environment because they are used globally in a long-term manner. Usually, these products take years and even decades of research and an infinite flow of investments. Just as with any invention or innovation project, the results are not certain. Hence, the Innovator usually takes great risks when embarking on a major research project.

Innovators are usually from the chemical/bio-technology/energy/high-tech industries because these capabilities are needed to invent and produce such products. Like Chad Holliday of DuPont, GE's Jeff Immelt is also embracing the green movement. He drives the company's efforts to develop everything from energy-saving light bulbs to desalination technology that improves clean water capacity.[3] Other companies that are playing an innovator role include Toyota with its hybrid cars, Dow Chemical and its biotechnology investments, and Empress La Moderna, a booming life-sciences company focusing on "green chemistry" research to find biological substitutes for synthetic chemicals.

For the Innovators, innovating for sustainable, environment-saving products forms the core of their raison d'être. That becomes the mission. The Innovator embraces what Walley and Whitehead stated in their *Harvard Business Review* article, "It's Not Easy Being Green": "Being green . . . is a catalyst for innovation."[4]

The Investor: Wal-Mart Case

There is also a change occurring in the world's largest retailer, Wal-Mart.[5] Known in the past for its oblivious attitude toward societal and environmental concerns, Wal-Mart has never rated high as a good corporate citizen. Wal-Mart was often criticized for its low wages and its frequent ignorance of environment issues. Robert Greenwald created a film entitled, *Wal-Mart: The High Cost of Low Price.* In that movie, there is a section highlighting the commentary of one veteran activist who said that she had never come across a corporation as ignorant as Wal-Mart. Even when it cost Wal-Mart millions of dollars in fines for its environmental abuse, the company continued to appear ignorant.

About 8 percent of consumers discontinued their regular shopping visit to Wal-Mart stores because they perceived the company negatively, according to a leaked McKinsey survey. In an attempt to ward off excessive negative publicity and finally address environmental issues, Wal-Mart proclaimed in 2005 that it would become a good steward of the environment. Wal-Mart's former CEO, Scott Lee, announced in his "21st Century Leadership" speech that Wal-Mart would spend hundreds of millions of dollars to redesign its business model with fuel-efficient processes and good waste management. With this new design, he expected greater efficiency gains to cover the costs.

To achieve this objective, Wal-Mart built green super-centers and introduced green labeled products in its stores. Given its size, Wal-Mart had become the largest retailer of organic milk and sustainable fish in the world in approximately just one year. Wal-Mart had also leveraged its strong bargaining position to force suppliers to find more efficient packaging and processes.

Many are excited about Wal-Mart's ambitious plans because a small transformation in one of the biggest companies in the world means a big change. The changes have also improved its PR as critics now have more favorable views on Wal-Mart's approach to social responsibility. However, many critics still say that Wal-Mart, whose classic tagline "Always Low Prices," drives its business model to only care about costs. Today, the tagline reads "Save money. Live better." But many see Wal-Mart's move to save the environment as being chiefly performed for selfish economic goals—to save energy, save costs, and increase revenue from increasing demand for green products.

By definition, the Investor is someone who "puts [money] to use, by purchase or expenditure, in something offering potential profitable returns, as interest, income, or appreciation in value."[6] Although this description may hint at being somewhat negative, especially in the context of giving something back to Mother Nature and not taking more, we do not mean for the Investor to be contributing less than the Innovator.

Investors are companies and individuals that finance research projects (usually by Innovators) in external companies or their own companies. For example, Wal-Mart invested

$500 million in 2005 so that its stores can use less energy, its trucks emit less poisonous gas, and so on.[7] Just like an Investor, Wal-Mart has calculated the costs and benefits and risks prior to its investment. Others belonging to the group of Investors are Goldman Sachs and Hewlett-Packard. Some manufacturers are also starting to invest to reduce their factories' gas emissions, reduce use of energy from their stores/computers, and so on.

The Investor will not take big risks in environmental efforts like the Innovator because the green business is not its core business mission. However, Investors share the vision of a greener and sustainable world. Besides seeking financial returns, the Investor also seeks returns in other areas—improvement in image, increase in brand value, avoidance of more pressure from environmental organizations, and selling green products to meet market demand, just to name a few. While Investors are not directly in the product innovation business, they make a major contribution by lending financial resources to support environmentally friendly projects.

The Propagator: Timberland Case

In contrast to Wal-Mart, Timberland is one of the most respected companies by all stakeholders. The global leader in the design, engineering, and marketing of premium-quality footwear, apparel, and accessories for consumers who value the outdoors, it believes in "doing well by doing good." It has not only been an environmentally-friendly company, but has created awareness about the environment among communities all over the world. It is especially known for its consistency in performing environmentally-friendly activities even through business down cycles.

In the production and promotion of its shoes, Timberland adheres strictly to a green business model. It uses recycled and nonchemical materials extensively in energy-efficient manufacturing processes. Inspired by the nutrition facts on food labels, it has introduced a "nutrition label" on each pair of shoes. The label provides consumers details "about the product they are purchasing, including where it was manufactured, how it was produced, and its effect on the environment."[8]

Timberland is very much focused on giving back to the communities in which it operates. With programs such as the Path of Service, Service Sabbaticals, Earth Day, and Serv-a-palooza, Timberland aims to help underprivileged communities as well as to promote its trademark values, including that of protecting the environment. Under the Path of Service program, Timberland employees have contributed over half a million hours of service around the world. That commitment has helped hundreds of community organizations in dozens of cities. Many of Timberland's activities involve protecting the environment. During Earth Day, for instance, Timberland planted a tree for each consumer who spent $150 on Timberland products.[9] Timberland has also done internal marketing activities such as providing incentives to employees to purchase hybrid cars.

The Propagator is usually a smaller size company in a non-chemical/biotechnology/energy/high-tech industry. The core differentiation usually lies in its green business model, which turns its internal values into external competitive advantage. The Propagator's mission, other than business, is to create awareness among user groups, employees, and the public about the importance of protecting the environment. It forms the critical mass or the support system that will purchase the products sold by the Innovator and which will support and appreciate the positive contribution of the Investor. Most importantly, Propagators seek to create environmental ambassadors by spreading the values of protecting the earth to employees and consumers.

The common strategy used to create environmental ambassadors is to create awareness in communities. Timberland illustrates the role of the Propagator best. Timberland seeks to inform, inspire, and engage. This is reflected clearly on its web site at www.timberlandserve.com.

Another strategy is bringing attention to the environment through its products. Timberland's new initiative—what it calls a nutritional label for shoes and boots—is an example. The innovative label tells all about the social and environmental impact that a person makes when buying shoes. While nutrition facts point to the impact of food on your wellness, Timberland's labels describe the impact of products on the earth's wellness. All the volunteer programs are reported through this new medium as well.[10]

Examples of other notable companies in this category are Patagonia, Whole Foods Market, Fetzer Vineyards, and Herman Miller. These companies are well-known for their environmental stewardship in creating more environmentally-friendly business practices.

THE COLLABORATION OF THE INNOVATOR, THE INVESTOR, AND THE PROPAGATOR

Because they have different motivations, the Innovators, the Investors, and the Propagators play their own unique roles in saving the environment. As described in *Green to Gold*, there are several motivations for companies that are moving toward a greener stance.[11]

1. Natural resources dependence
2. Current exposure to regulation
3. Increasing potential for regulation
4. Competitive market for talent
5. Low market power in a highly competitive market
6. Good environmental track records
7. High brand exposure
8. Big environmental impact

Reasons 1 to 3 are the main motivations for the Innovators, reasons 4 to 6 for the Propagators, and reasons 7 to 8 for the Investors (see Figure 9.1).

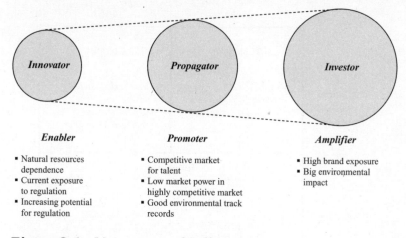

Figure 9.1 Motivations of Different Actors

Both Investors and Propagators promote the environmental cause through their business processes, whereas Innovators produce products that are environmentally friendly. Propagators play in niche markets whereas Investors play in more mass markets. To create reinforcements of impacts, all three types should exist in the market. The buzz is started by the Propagators, which build their competitive advantage from their concern about the environment. This buzz builds up public opinion for the environmental cause. However, Propagators like Whole Foods Market will take a longer time to bring green products into the mainstream. Without influence from Investors like Wal-Mart, green products will remain exclusive to a niche market. Propagators also need Innovators to supply them with innovative green products (see Figure 9.2).

TARGETING COMMUNITIES FOR GREEN MARKETING

It is important to recognize that the green market is far from homogeneous. The market for green products and services can be classified into four segments: trendsetters, value-seekers, standard matchers, and cautious buyers. Trendsetters are the early market whereas value-seekers and standard matchers are the mainstream market and the cautious buyers

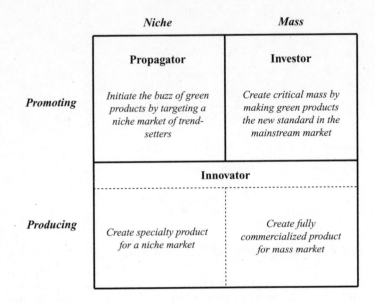

Figure 9.2 Collaboration of Different Actors

are laggards. Because each segment has different sets of beliefs toward product benefit, the marketing approach for each segment should be different. As for the cautious buyers, it is better not to pursue them. See Table 9.1.

Trendsetters are the most important segments in the introduction stage of a green product. They become not only the first customers to adopt the product but also the important influencers in the market. Make them promoters who will recommend and endorse the products to their friends and families.

Based on the VALS,[12] trendsetters can be classified in the Innovators segment. They are change leaders and are the most receptive to new ideas and technologies. They are very active consumers, and their purchases reflect sophisticated tastes for upscale, niche products and services. However, green products will not take off to the growth stage if they remain in the niche market of tree huggers. As long as green products are the exclusive domain of well-off people,

Table 9.1 Four Segments of the Green Market

	Customer Segmentation			
	Trendsetter	Value-seeker	Standard matcher	Cautious buyer
Segment Profile	- Tree hugger or visionary environmental enthusiast - Emotional and spiritual motivation for using green product - Looking for competitive advantage through green innovation	- Environmental pragmatist - Rational motivation for using green products - Utilizing green products to increase efficiency and save costs	- Environmental conservative - Wait and see for green products to reach mass usage - Using green products that have already became standard	- Environmental skeptics - Do not believe in green products
Positioning for Targeting the Segment	*Eco-advantage* *Innovative product for competitive advantage*	*Eco-efficiency* *More value with less impact*	*Eco-standard* *Product with mass usage and conformance*	*Not worth pursuing*

their benefits will be limited. To have an impact, they should be widely accepted in the marketplace. That's why major corporations are greening their mainstream brands. Take Tide Coldwater, which is formulated to wash clothes best in cold water.[13]

Unlike the trendsetter market, which is more emotional and spiritual, the mainstream market is more rational when it comes to buying green products. The value-seeker segment buys green products if they are cost-efficient. Consumers of this type would not pay more to be green. Therefore, green products must be affordable when targeting this segment. Marketers should also be able to point out the cost-savings from using green products.

People who are classified as "thinkers" in VALS are the key target market. They are open to considering new ideas. They are a type of customer who can easily be influenced away from bad decisions and toward more responsible ones. Therefore, marketers should design programs that give them options but steer them away from the bad ones.[14] Communicating greener product options in addition to regular ones will lead value-seekers to choose the better options.

However, value-seekers are also conservative, practical consumers; they look for durability, functionality, and value in the products they buy. To engage this segment, green marketers need to put an emphasis on how their product will provide more value with less environmental impact. Therefore, the marketing communication should be themed around the concept of eco-efficiency.

While value-seekers are practical, the standard-matchers are more conservative. They do not buy a product that is not yet a standard in an industry. The product's popularity is the most important reason to buy. To appeal to this segment, the green product has to reach the critical mass to be considered a standard. It is imperative to have a catalyst. For example, the rise of environmentally-friendly buildings has been largely driven by the development of green building standards. This was pioneered by the U.K. government and followed by the U.S. government. More and more countries such as Australia

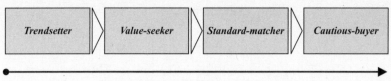

Decreased likelihood of buying green products

Figure 9.3   The Market Segment Influence Chain

and India are developing their own green building standards. These trends are moving green buildings into mainstream markets.[15]

The cautious buyers, the fourth segment, are the customers who are so skeptical that they avoid buying green products although greener business is already an accepted belief. This type of customer is too costly to pursue and convert.

To lead a product across its life cycle means to lead the product across the market segment influence chain (see Figure 9.3). In the introduction stage, marketers need to use green as a key source of differentiation. However, marketers need to use word-of-mouth marketing to create hype and a snowball effect to reach the growth stage. According to *Crossing the Chasm* by Geoffrey Moore, there is a gap in the market—the chasm—that separates the early market from the mainstream market.[16] Green products have to cross the chasm and become popular. Once a product reaches the maturity stage, competition intensifies and marketers need to start finding differentiators other than just being green. (See Figure 9.4.)

SUMMARY: GREEN INNOVATION FOR SUSTAINABILITY

In this chapter, we underscore the importance of values-based companies moving toward a green commitment. Benefits include lower cost, better reputation, and more motivated employees. Companies such as DuPont contribute to the green movement by playing the role of Innovator. Companies such as Wal-Mart contribute by playing the role of Investor. And

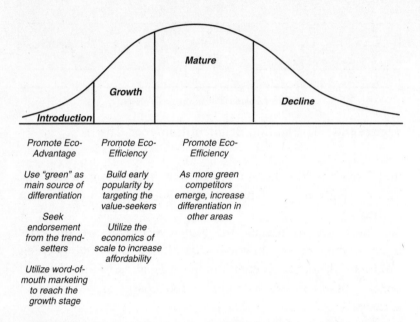

Figure 9.4 The Life Cycle of Creating Green Awareness and Purchase

Timberland contributes by playing the role of Propagator. Having examined the characteristics of these different roles, we argue that when they all operate in the same market and collaborate, that the green market will be reinforced. Finally, companies need to distinguish the four segments in the green market—the trendsetters, value-seekers, standard matchers, and cautious buyers and note their differing behaviors and readiness to buy green products. Companies that promote environmental sustainability are practicing Marketing 3.0.

NOTES

1. The DuPont Case is mainly written based on an article by Nicholas Varchaver, "Chemical Reaction," *Fortune*, March 22, 2007.
2. Stuart L. Hart, "Beyond Greening: Strategies for a Sustainable World," *Harvard Business Review*, January–February 1997.

3. Marc Gunther, "Green is Good," *Fortune Magazine*, March 22, 2007.

4. Noah Walley and Bradley Whitehead, "It's Not Easy Being Green," *Harvard Business Review*, May–June 1994.

5. The Wal-Mart Case is mainly written based on an article by Marc Gunther, "The Green Machine," *Fortune*, July 31, 2006.

6. From www.dictionary.com.

7. "Is Wal-Mart Going Green?" *MSNBC News Services*, October 25, 2005.

8. Timberland homepage, www.timberland.com, May 11, 2007.

9. Jayne O'Donnell and Christine Dugas, "More Retailers Go for Green—the Eco Kind," *USA Today*, April 19, 2007.

10. Marc Gunther, "Compassionate Capitalism at Timberland," *Fortune*, February 8, 2006.

11. Daniel C. Esty and Andrew S. Winston, *Green to Gold: How Smart Companies Use Environmental Strategy to Innovate, Create Value, and Build Competitive Advantage* (New Haven, CT: Yale University Press, 2006).

12. VALS is the system that identifies current and future opportunities by segmenting the consumer marketplace on the basis of the personality traits that drive consumer behavior. See www.sric-bi.com/VALS/ for a more detailed description of the segmentation.

13. Anne Underwood, "10 Fixes for the Planet," *Newsweek*, May 5, 2008.

14. Read more about how to nudge customers toward more responsible options in Richard H. Thaler and Cass R. Sunstein, *Nudge: Improving Decisions about Health, Wealth, and Happiness* (New Haven, CT: Yale University Press, 2008).

15. Charles Lockwood, "Building the Green Way," *Harvard Business Review*, June 2006.

16. Geoffrey A. Moore, *Crossing the Chasm: Marketing and Selling High Tech to Mainstream Customers* (New York: HarperBusiness, 1999).

CHAPTER TEN

Putting It All Together

10 CREDOS OF MARKETING 3.0

There are three stages in the development of a relationship between marketing and values. The first is when marketing and values are *polarized*. Many businesspeople believe that marketing does not require that you adopt a set of high-minded values. If you do, living up to the values will just impose extra costs and constraints. Subsequently, a second stage arises that we call *balancing*. Businesses then do marketing in the ordinary way, donating some of their profits to social causes. Then there is the third stage, that of *integration*. This is the ultimate stage. The company wants to live out a set of values, and these values give the company its personality and purpose. Any separation between marketing and values is not acceptable.

Once we look more deeply at marketing's roots and more fully comprehend them, we discover 10 indisputable credos that integrate marketing and values. For each credo, we will mention some companies that have applied the credo in the way they do marketing. Some companies do it through their contributions to United Nations Millennium Development Goals (MDGs), the eight time-bound and measurable goals and targets agreed to by 189 world leaders in September 2000 at the United Nations Millennium Summit.[1]

The Millennium Development Goals are as follows.

1. Eradicate extreme poverty and hunger.
2. Achieve universal primary education.
3. Promote gender equality and empower women.
4. Reduce child mortality.
5. Improve maternal health.
6. Combat HIV/AIDS, malaria, and other diseases.
7. Ensure environmental sustainability.
8. Develop a global partnership for development.

MDGs began as a government-to-government initiative. However, corporations are starting to see the business side of the goals. Unilever, Procter & Gamble, Holcim, Philips, Vodafone, S.C. Johnson, BP, ConocoPhilips, and Rabobank to name a few, are big companies that are already making profits from incorporating the goals into their operations in developing countries. These companies demonstrate how they make a difference to the world and how the difference redounds to their monetary and nonmonetary benefit. Some of the cases in this chapter are taken from *Business for Development: Business Solutions in Support of the Millennium Development Goals* to show the linkage between Marketing 3.0 and the effort toward achieving the MDGs.[2]

CREDO 1: LOVE YOUR CUSTOMERS, RESPECT YOUR COMPETITORS

In business, loving your customers means winning their loyalty through giving them great value and touching their emotions and spirit. Remember what Donald Calne said: "The essential difference between emotion and reason is that emotion leads to actions while reason leads to conclusions."[3] The decision to buy and be loyal to a brand is greatly influenced by emotions.

Campbell Soup Company, for instance, changed the color of its packaging to pink during Breast Cancer Awareness Month and managed to improve demand significantly.[4] Since typical soup consumers are women and breast cancer is a cause many women are emotionally connected to, sales to women went up. This example shows that emphasizing emotion over reason does pay off.

Furthermore, you have to respect your competitors. It is competitors that enlarge the whole market, because without any competitors, an industry will grow more slowly. From monitoring our competitors, we can learn our own strengths and weaknesses as well as those of competitors; something that can prove very useful for our company.

The strategy of growing the market by allowing competition to happen can be done through vertical or horizontal technology transfers. Look at Unilever in Vietnam, for example.[5] Unilever provides training of best practices to all local suppliers. During training, suppliers learn about standard quality and the necessary technology to achieve this standard. Not only that, Unilever also provides financial support to the suppliers. By doing this, Unilever is able to maintain low cost from local suppliers and manage quality at the same time. One thing to consider is the possibility of Unilever's suppliers serving competitors. And interestingly, Unilever allows that to happen because it helps to develop the overall market.

On the other hand, horizontal technology transfer is even more difficult to comprehend. Not many companies are willing to transfer their technology to competitors directly. But this is possible when a company feels that it is incapable of growing the market alone.[6] Such a company wants to share the risk. It needs alliances to achieve economies of scale. A prominent example is the cooperation of seven pharmaceutical companies (Boehringer Ingelheim, Bristol-Myers Squibb, GlaxoSmithKline, Merck, Roche, Abbot, and Gilead) that collaboratively brought down the price of HIV/AIDS treatment in developing countries in pursuit of MDGs.[7]

Another example is when multiple telecommunications companies in the United Kingdom (Motorola, Carphone Warehouse, O2, Orange, Vodafone, T-Mobile, Tesco, Virgin Mobile, and Fresh) collaborated with Bono and Bobby Shriver to introduce a new RED mobile phone designed to help fight AIDS in Africa. Tens of millions of pounds for AIDS treatment and prevention was raised from this launch.[8]

Treat your customers with love and your competitors with respect.

CREDO 2: BE SENSITIVE TO CHANGE, BE READY TO TRANSFORM

The business landscape keeps changing. Competitors will increase in number and get smarter. The same goes for customers. If you are insensitive to this and cannot anticipate these changes, your company will become obsolete and eventually die.

Before Prius, Toyota was never considered a disruptive innovator that relied on breakthrough products.[9] Instead, the company was known for its continuous innovation combined with its slow-but-sure decision making process. However, Toyota sensed the trends in the market and realized that it had to introduce a hybrid car quickly before it became obsolete. Thus, in introducing the Prius, it broke many of its strict Japanese management systems and acted quickly in product development.

Even Wal-Mart, the retail giant, cannot avoid transforming itself.[10] The world's largest retailer has been criticized for many things and attacked by many for its employment, environmental, and supply chain practices. In the past few years, the company has transformed itself into a green giant. Wal-Mart finally realized that the low price strategy that made it a winner might not work in the future as consumer behavior changed.

When times change, change with them.

CREDO 3: GUARD YOUR NAME,
BE CLEAR ABOUT WHO YOU ARE

In marketing, brand reputation is everything. If two products are of equal quality, people will tend to purchase the one that has the stronger brand reputation. A company must make its brand name's positioning and differentiation clear to its target market.

The Body Shop is one of the world's leading examples of a values-driven business. The British company's prominent practice of community trade—buying natural ingredients from local and poor communities around the world—is probably the best sourcing know-how that attempts to eradicate poverty at the same time.

Another business practice that The Body Shop is famous for is its commitment to opposition of animal testing. The progressive company has forbidden the testing of its products on animals long before a regulation was enforced in the EU. These unusual practices are neither efficient nor make common business sense, for sure. Nevertheless, they have helped The Body Shop to become one of the United Kingdom's most successful retailers by creating a niche market for naturally-inspired products.

As a result, the world's largest cosmetic company, L'Oreal, acquired the company in a phenomenal deal worth a premium of 34.2 percent. The challenge for The Body Shop is to guard its name externally while internally influencing L'Oreal—a company that has been criticized for testing certain ingredients on animals—to strengthen its business values.

Make your values clear and don't surrender them.

CREDO 4: CUSTOMERS ARE DIVERSE; GO FIRST TO
THOSE WHO CAN BENEFIT MOST FROM YOU

This is the principle of segmentation. You do not need to address everyone, but do make your case to those who are most ready to buy and benefit from the purchase and relationship.

Most product markets comprise four distinct tiers.[11]

1. A global segment that desires global products and features and is willing to pay higher prices for them.
2. A "glocal" segment that demands products of global quality but with local features at slightly lower prices.
3. A local segment that wants local products with local features at local prices.
4. A bottom-of-the-pyramid segment that can afford to buy only the cheapest products available.

The bottom-of-the-pyramid segment is the appropriate segment for local companies to challenge their multinational rivals in developing countries. It is also the appropriate segment for Marketing 3.0.

Holcim is addressing the need of the poor for affordable housing in Sri Lanka. The company collaborated with a microfinance company to build shop houses: homes that are designed to be places to run small businesses as well. Holcim sees these low-income consumers as the future market as they climb up the economic pyramid. On the other hand, this project transforms the community by providing better houses and giving poor people access to a source of income. For that reason, it helps achieve Goals 1, 2, 3, 7, and 8 of MDGs.[12]

Focus on those to whom you can bring the most benefit.

CREDO 5: ALWAYS OFFER A GOOD PACKAGE AT A FAIR PRICE

We should not sell anything of poor quality at a high price. True marketing is fair marketing, where price and product must match. Once we seek to cheat people by giving them a poor quality product but representing it as a good quality product, our customers will abandon us.

Unilever tries to bring down the price of iodized salt so that it can replace the noniodized salt heavily used in Ghana.

To improve the health of the local community, Unilever uses its global capability. With experience in consumer product marketing, Unilever brings affordability through sachet marketing. The backbone of this effort is Unilever's application of its expertise in supply chain to reduce the distribution costs. This project specifically targets Goals 1, 2, and 5 of the MDGs.[13]

Another example is Procter & Gamble's effort to provide safe drinking water. Like Unilever, the company is equipped with expertise in sachet marketing. With its proprietary water-treatment technology, the company delivers safe water around the world. Interestingly, the technology is in a size of a sachet to ensure affordability. Local people can pour the content of the sachet to clean 10 liters of water for drinking. With this effort, the company is helping the world to achieve Goals 5, 6, and 10 of the MDGs.[14]

Set fair prices to reflect your quality.

CREDO 6: ALWAYS MAKE YOURSELF AVAILABLE, SPREAD THE GOOD NEWS

Don't make it hard for customers who are looking for you to find you. In today's global knowledge economy, access to information technology and the Internet is imperative. But the digital divide—the socio-cultural differences between those who have access to digital technology and the Internet and those who don't—is still a challenge around the world. Companies that can straddle the divide will grow their consumer base.

Since 2005, Hewlett-Packard has been trying to bridge the divide by collaborating with partners across sectors to bring information technology to developing nations.[15] In pursuit of growth, the company targets the low-income communities as its future market. In the process of market creation, it progressively bridges the digital divide and provides poor people with access to technology. These consumers are the hope for companies in mature markets that seek growth.

Help your would-be customers find you.

CREDO 7: GET YOUR CUSTOMERS, KEEP AND GROW THEM

Once you have a customer, keep up good relations with them. Get to know your customers personally, one by one, so you have a complete picture of their needs and wants and preferences and behavior. Then grow their business. These are the principles of customer relationship management (CRM). It is about attracting the right customers who will keep buying from you because of deep rational and emotional satisfaction. They are also capable of becoming your strongest advocates through word-of-mouth marketing.

PetSmart Charities has saved the lives of millions of homeless pets through its in-store adoption centers.[16] The program brings visitors to the stores and improves the sales of Pet-Smart products. While helping the pets, the company attracts new customers and cross-sells to them at the point-of-sale. Because the company demonstrates its care for pets, consumers will be touched and become loyal.

Look upon your customers as customers for life.

CREDO 8: WHATEVER YOUR BUSINESS, IT IS A SERVICE BUSINESS

Service businesses are not limited to hotels or restaurants. Whatever your business, you must have a spirit of wanting to serve your customer. Service must become a service provider's calling, and never be considered a duty. Serve your customer sincerely and with complete empathy, as they will assuredly then carry away positive memories from this experience. Companies should understand that their corporate values, expressed through their products and services, should have a positive impact on people's lives.

Whole Foods sees its business as service to consumers and service to society. That is why the company tries to transform the lifestyles of consumers into healthier ones. Moreover, it is practicing the sense of service to employees as well by letting them vote on the company's strategic direction.

Every business is a service business, because every product delivers a service.

CREDO 9: ALWAYS REFINE YOUR BUSINESS PROCESS IN TERMS OF QUALITY, COST, AND DELIVERY

The task of marketers is to always improve quality, cost, and delivery (QCD) in their business processes. Always meet all your promises to customers, suppliers, and to your channels, too. Never engage in deceit or dishonesty with regard to quality, quantity, delivery time, or price.

S.C. Johnson is well-known for doing business with local suppliers. It works with local farmers to improve productivity and delivery. To maintain a sustainable supply of Pyrethrum, for instance, the company engages the local farmers in Kenya. In partnership with KickStart and the Pyrethrum Board of Kenya, the company helps the farmers with irrigation. Farmers achieve higher productivity with new irrigation pumps and therefore can better supply S.C. Johnson. Furthermore, the farmers get additional income because the pump enables them to plant other crops. While improving the supply chain of the company, S.C. Johnson contributes to Goals 1, 2, and 6 of MDGs directly and indirectly.[17]

Every day, improve your business process in every way.

CREDO 10: GATHER RELEVANT INFORMATION, BUT USE WISDOM IN MAKING YOUR FINAL DECISION

This principle cautions us to continually learn, learn, and learn. Your accumulated knowledge and experience will be what determines the final decision you make. Supported by his or her maturity of spirit and clarity of heart, a marketer will then be able to swiftly make decisions based on the wisdom that they inherently have.

An interesting story about Hershey Foods in *The Triple Bottom Line* by Andrew Savitz and Karl Weber describes this.[18] In 2001, the board members of Hershey Trust considered selling its stake in Hershey Foods because of the emergence of a powerful competitor in the market and a likely future large increase in the price of cocoa. From a financial perspective, these would decrease the value of the trust fund that the board maintained. To guard its pursuit of maximum shareholder value, the board of trustees sold its entire stake to Wrigley.

To the board's surprise, a group of angry employees refused this acquisition. They rallied and then gathered on Chocolatetown Square to protest the sale. The board finally realized its decision was wrong. Financially, the decision was sound. However, it was not wise because it didn't consider the social impact of the decision, especially to the employees.

Wise managers consider more than the financial impact of a decision.

MARKETING 3.0: IT'S TIME TO MAKE A CHANGE!

Is it possible to be a human-centric company and still be profitable? This book offers a positive answer to this question. The behavior and values of a company are increasingly open to public inspection. The growth of social networks makes it feasible and easier for people to talk about existing companies, products, and brands in terms of their functional performance as well as their social performance. The new generation of consumers is much more attuned to social issues and concerns. Companies must reinvent themselves and shift as swiftly as possible from practicing in the formerly safe confines of Marketing 1.0 and 2.0 into the new world of Marketing 3.0.

NOTES

1. For more information about MDGs, see www.un.org/millennium goals/.
2. Cécile Churet & Amanda Oliver, *Business for Development: Business Solutions in Support of the Millennium Development Goals*, World Business Council for Sustainable Development, 2005.

3. Donald B. Calne, *Within Reason: Rationality and Human Behavior* (New York: Pantheon Books, 1999).

4. Stephanie Thompson, "Breast Cancer Awareness Strategy Increases Sales of Campbell's Soup: Pink-Labeled Cans a Hit with Kroger Customers," *AdvertisingAge*, October 3, 2006.

5. Sébastien Miroudot, "The Linkages between Open Services Market and Technology Transfer," OECD Trade Policy Working Paper No. 29, January 27, 2006.

6. Adam M. Brandenburger and Barry J. Nalebuff, *Co-opetition: A Revolutionary Mindset that Combines Competition and Cooperation... The Game Theory Strategy that's Changing the Game of Business* (New York: Currency Doubleday, 1996).

7. "Increasing People's Access to Essential Medicines in Developing Countries: A Framework for Good Practice in the Pharmaceutical Industry," A UK Government Policy Paper, Department for International Development, March 2005.

8. Martin Hickman, "(RED) Phone Unites Rival Telecom Operators in Battle against AIDS," *The Independent*, May 16, 2006.

9. Alex Taylor III, "Toyota: The Birth of the Prius," *Fortune*, February 21, 2006.

10. Marc Gunther, "The Green Machine," *Fortune*, July 31, 2006.

11. Tarun Khanna and Krishna G. Palepu, "Emerging Giants: Building World-Class Companies in Developing Countries," *Harvard Business Review*, October 2006.

12. Cécile Churet & Amanda Oliver, *Op.Cit.*

13. Cécile Churet & Amanda Oliver, *Op.Cit.*

14. Cécile Churet & Amanda Oliver, *Op.Cit.*

15. Ira A. Jackson and Jane Nelson, *Profit with Principles: Seven Strategies for Delivering Value with Values* (New York: Currency Doubleday, 2004).

16. Philip Kotler and Nancy Lee, *Corporate Social Responsibility: Doing the Most Good for Your Company and Your Cause* (Hoboken, NJ: John Wiley & Sons, 2005).

17. Cécile Churet & Amanda Oliver, *Op.Cit.*

18. Andrew W. Savitz and Karl Weber, *The Triple Bottom Line: How Today's Best-Run Companies Are Achieving Economic, Social, and Environmental Success—and How You Can Too* (San Francisco: Jossey-Bass, 2006).

INDEX